PEARSON LONGMAN

PEARSON English Learning System

Teacher's Resource Book

Anna Uhl Chamot

Jim Cummins

Sharroky Hollie

PEARSON

Upper Saddle River, New Jersey • Boston, Massachusetts • Chandler, Arizona • Glenview, Illinois

Pearson Longman Cornerstone 3
Teacher's Resource Book

PEARSON English Learning System

Staff credits: The people who made up the Longman Cornerstone team, representing editorial, production, design, manufacturing, and marketing, are John Ade, Rhea Banker, Daniel Comstock, David Dickey, Gina DiLillo, Johnnie Farmer, Nancy Flaggman, Charles Green, Karen Kawaguchi, Ed Lamprich, Niki Lee, Jaime Leiber, Chris Leonowicz, Tara Maceyak, Linda Moser, Laurie Neaman, Leslie Patterson, Sherri Pemberton, Liza Pleva, Susan Saslow, Chris Siley, Loretta Steeves, Kim Steiner, and Lauren Weidenman.
Text composition: The Quarasan Group, Inc.

ISBN-13: 978-0-328-73794-9
ISBN-10: 0-328-73794-1

Printed in the United States of America
2 3 4 5 6 7 8 9 10 V056 16 15

Contents

LESSON PLANS

The chart below provides a legend for the Common Core State Standards abbreviations used in the Lesson Plans. For the full text of the standards, refer to Appendix A in the *Teacher's Edition*.

Abbreviation	Skill Strand or Subject Area
RL	Reading standards for literature
RI	Reading standards for informational text
RF	Reading standards for foundational skills
W	Writing standards
SL	Speaking and listening standards
L	Language standards

Lesson 1

Common Core State Standards: RI.3.7, SL.3.1, SL.3.1.c, SL.3.6

Unit Opener *Student Book* pages 2–3
- Use *Transparencies* 1 for Daily Language Practice, Week 1, Day 1.
- Have students complete the Diagnostic Pretest in the *Assessments* to determine students' initial levels of ability.

Unit: Communities Introduce the theme. Discuss the meaning of the word *communities*. Build students' background on the unit theme by presenting the poster and the video.
Fluency Activity Post the Unit 1 Poster on the wall. Do Fluency Activity 1 at the bottom of TE page T2.
Visual Literacy Have students look at the numbered pictures at the bottom of page 2. Tell them that the labels above the pictures tell what type of reading each selection is and that the labels under the pictures are the titles of the selections.
The Big Question Ask students how communities may be alike and different.
Listening and Speaking Read aloud the text and ask students to name activities they do in their communities. Write a list of their words on the board and pronounce them.
Writing Read the text aloud and tell students that they will do this later in the unit.
Quick Write Read the activity aloud, and have students write three sentences. Ask volunteers to share their sentences.

Homework
Ask students to take the Letter Home to their parents, explain it to them, and have their parents sign it.

Lesson 2

Common Core State Standards: RL.3.4, RI.3.4, RI.3.7, W.3.5, W.3.10, SL.3.1, SL.3.1.c, SL.3.6, L.3.4, L.3.4.a, L.3.5.b, L.3.4.d, L.3.6

What do you know about communities? *Student Book* pages 4–5
- Use *Transparencies* 1 for Daily Language Practice, Week 1, Day 2.

Words to Know Say each of the terms on pages 4–5. Encourage students to point to the correct illustration as they repeat each term with you. Have students work in pairs to do the Practice activity on page 4. Students ask and answer the questions using the new words on the page. Ask students to complete the Write activity independently and share their answer with their partner.
Make Connections Have students work in pairs to complete the activity. Have pairs combine with other pairs to check their answers.
What About You? Have students discuss the question with a partner. Encourage them to use the words they learned on these pages.

Homework
Have students answer the What About You questions in their notebooks.

Lesson 3

Common Core State Standards: RI.3.7, SL.3.1, SL.3.1.c, SL.3.6

Kids' Stories from Around the World *Student Book* pages 6–7
- Use *Transparencies* 3 for Daily Language Practice, Week 1, Day 3.

Kids' Stories from Around the World Read the children's stories. Students can also listen to the peer stories on the Audio CD.

Visual Literacy Draw students' attention to the map of the world. Have students follow the lines from the photos of each child's home to its location on the map. Say the name of each location, and have students repeat the locations aloud. Encourage students to use other world maps or globes to find the same places.

What About You? Have students discuss different communities in both your area and other parts of the U.S. Talk about activities they can do in these communities. Have students share stories about how they get to school.

Fluency Activity Do Fluency Activity 2 at the bottom of TE page T6.

Homework
Have students write about special places in their community.

Lesson 4

Common Core State Standards: RL.3.4, SL.3.1, SL.3.1.c, SL.3.6, L.3.4, L.3.4.a, L.3.5.b

Reading 1 Key Words   *Student Book* pages 8–9
• Use *Transparencies* 1 for Daily Language Practice, Week 1, Day 4.
• Use *Transparencies* 37 for Key Words.

Prepare to Read Draw students' attention to the What You Will Learn section. Briefly discuss the topics that will be covered in this reading.

Key Words Read the key words aloud or play them on the Audio CD. Have students repeat each word as it is read aloud.

Words in Context Help students learn the skill of defining words by using context to define the highlighted words.

Visual Literacy Have students find the numbers next to the sentences on pages 8–9 and then find the corresponding numbered photos.

Practice Read the text in the *Student Book* and have students complete the activity.

Apply Read the text aloud. Have students work in pairs to discuss the questions. Circulate and encourage students to use key words in their responses.

Fluency Activity Do Fluency Activity 3 at the bottom of TE page T8.

Homework
Have students complete the Key Words activities on *Workbook* page 3.

Lesson 5

Common Core State Standards: RI.3.4, RF.3.3, SL.3.1, SL.3.1.c, SL.3.6, L.3.4, L.3.4.a

Academic Words & Phonics   *Student Book* pages 10–11
• Use *Transparencies* 1 for Daily Language Practice, Week 1, Day 5.

Academic Words Discuss the definitions of the words and have students listen to the words in context on the Audio CD. Have students complete the Practice activity in their notebooks.

Apply Have students try to use the academic words when discussing the questions with a partner.

Phonics Play the Audio CD to show students the phonics pattern. Discuss the rule and ask students if they can think of other words that follow the same pattern. Have students complete the Practice section with a partner.

Homework
Have students complete the Academic Words and Phonics practice on *Workbook* pages 4–5.

Lesson 6

Common Core State Standards: RL.3.1, RL.3.3, RL.3.4, RL.3.7, RL.3.10, L.3.4, L.3.4.a, L.3.5.a, L.3.6

Reading 1 *Student Book* pages 12–15

• Use *Transparencies* 2 for Daily Language Practice, Week 2, Day 1.

More About the Big Question Read aloud the Big Question on page 12. Have students think about the question as they read the poem. Encourage students to think about how their everyday actions affect other people.

Audio Play the audio of the poem, stopping to answer questions students may have. Discuss the general meaning of the poem and how it relates to the Big Question.

Reading Strategy Explain the term *character*. SAY *A* character *is a person or animal in a story or a poem. Characters do things. Things happen to characters. Who is the main character in the poem? Look at the pictures.* Read aloud the bulleted items on page 12.

Genre Draw students' attention to the genre. Tell students that poems often rhyme and this is one way to distinguish poems from other readings. Ask students to name the rhyming words at the ends of the lines.

Read Students can take turns reading the stanzas of the poem on pages 12–15. Encourage students to refer to the illustrations as they read.

Build Vocabulary Help students recognize how to use the word in bold type that is defined on the bottom of page 13. Invite a volunteer to read the word and its definition aloud. Have students make up sentences that use the word in context.

Key Words Discuss the yellow highlighted words in the poem and why they are key words for this reading.

Fluency Activity Do Fluency Activity 4 at the bottom of TE page T14.

Homework
Have students complete the Comprehension activities on page 6 of the *Workbook*.

Lesson 7

Common Core State Standards: RL.3.1, RL.3.3, RL.3.4, RL.3.7, RL.3.10, L.3.4, L.3.4.a, L.3.5.a, L.3.6

Reading 1 *Student Book* pages 12–15

• Use *Transparencies* 2 for Daily Language Practice, Week 2, Day 2.
• Have students complete the Reader's Companion on page 7 of the *Workbook*.

Read Students may reread the poem silently or follow along while listening to the Audio CD.

Reading Strategy After reading the poem, discuss what students have learned about Hector's character. Explain that *clues* are things that help you find answers. Ask students how Hector helps Ms. Rodriguez, and have students find other examples of Hector's friendly behavior.

Visual Literacy Draw the students' attention to the illustrations on pages 14–15. Ask volunteers to describe what is happening in each picture.

Respond Have students work in pairs or small groups to complete the Think It Over questions. Discuss the answer to the Analyze question. Encourage students to use the illustrations as evidence to support their opinions.

Fluency Activity Do Fluency Activity 5 on page 164 of the *TRB*.

Homework
Have students complete the Comprehension activities on *Workbook* page 8.

Lesson 8

Common Core State Standards: RL.3.2, RL.3.3, L.3.1.e, SL.3.6

Learning Strategies *Student Book* pages 16–17

- Use *Transparencies* 2 for Daily Language Practice, Week 2, Day 3.
- Use *Transparencies* 68 and page 154 of the *Teacher's Resource Book* for the Character Web.

More About the Big Question Discuss why each person is important to the community. Ask students to think of other important community members who were not in the poem.

Character Invite a class discussion. SAY *We learn things about a character from what he or she says and does. What kinds of things does Hector say in the poem? What does Hector do in the poem? What have you learned about Hector?* Let students know that words that tell what a character is like are called *character traits*.

Practice You may assign the Practice activity as a class discussion, partner activity, or individual written assignment.

Use a Character Web Copy the Character Web text into the circles on the transparency. Discuss how what Hector does in the poem tells what he is like. Have students complete the graphic organizer and share their answers.

Apply In pairs, have students retell the poem. Encourage students to use the illustrations to help them. Listen for use of key words and vocabulary in their retellings. Extension Have students discuss what they could draw in their pictures with a partner.

Homework
Have students complete the drawing from the Extension activity and do *Workbook* page 9.

Lesson 9

Common Core State Standards: L.3.1, L.3.1.d, L.3.1.e, SL.3.1, SL.3.1.c, SL.3.6

Grammar *Student Book* pages 18–19

- Use *Transparencies* 2 for Daily Language Practice, Week 2, Day 4.
- Have students complete the Unit 1, Reading 1 test in the *Assessments*.

Simple Present: *be* Verbs Read the introduction and refer to the chart to introduce the different forms of the verb *be*. Have volunteers say a sentence using each form.

Practice Have students work individually. Then have them form small groups and check their answers. Encourage them to refer to the chart as they do so.

Apply Have students work in pairs to ask and answer the questions, using different forms of *be*.

Homework
Have students complete the Grammar and Spelling exercises on *Workbook* pages 10–11.

Lesson 10

Common Core State Standards: W.3.2, W.3.2.a, W.3.4, W.3.5, W.3.10, SL.3.6

Writing *Student Book* pages 20–21

- Use *Transparencies* 2 for Daily Language Practice, Week 2, Day 5.
- Use *Transparencies* 63 and page 149 of the *Teacher's Resource Book* for the T-Chart.

Describe a Person Read aloud the text at the top of page 20. Refer to the Character Web describing Hector that students completed. Read aloud the Writing Prompt.

It may be helpful to complete the T-chart about Hector together before students begin Prewriting.

Prewrite Give the students copies of the T-Chart, or have them copy one into their notebooks. Encourage students to be specific about the things their person does. You may wish to brainstorm additional character traits or refer students to a general character traits list.

Draft Model how to turn the information in the T-Chart into a draft by writing a paragraph about Hector.

Writing Checklist Model how to use the Writing Checklist on page 21 to help you improve the paragraph you wrote about Hector. Encourage students to check for correct use of the verb *be*. Have students trade papers and do a Peer Review, using the Checklist on page 402.

Homework
Have students prepare a final copy of their paragraph and do *Workbook* page 12.

Lesson 11

Common Core State Standards: RL.3.4, RI.3.7, SL.3.1, SL.3.1.c, SL.3.6, L.3.2, L.3.4, L.3.4.a, L.3.5.b

Reading 2 Key Words   *Student Book* pages 22–23
- Use *Transparencies* 3 for Daily Language Practice, Week 3, Day 1.
- Use *Transparencies* 38 for Key Words.

Prepare to Read Draw students' attention to the What You Will Learn section. Briefly discuss the topics that will be covered in this reading.

Key Words Read the key words aloud or play them on the Audio CD. Have students repeat each word as it is read aloud.

Words in Context Help students learn the skill of defining words by using context to define the highlighted words.

Visual Literacy Have students find the numbered circles by the sentences on pages 22–23 and then find the corresponding numbered photos.

Practice Read the text in the *Student Book* and have students complete the activity. Give students time to practice using their flashcards with a partner.

Apply Read the text aloud. Have students work in pairs to discuss the questions. Circulate and encourage students to use key words in their responses.

Fluency Activity Do Fluency Activity 6 in TE on page T22.

Homework
Have students complete the Key Words practice on *Workbook* page 13.

Lesson 12

Common Core State Standards: RI.3.4, RF.3.3, SL.3.1, SL.3.1.c, SL.3.6, L.3.4, L.3.4.a

Academic Words & Phonics   *Student Book* pages 24–25
- Use *Transparencies* 3 for Daily Language Practice, Week 3, Day 2.

Academic Words Discuss the definitions of the words and have students listen to the words in context on the Audio CD. Have students complete the Practice activity in their notebooks.

Apply Have students use the academic words when discussing the questions in the Apply section with a partner.

Phonics Play the Audio CD to show students the phonics pattern. Discuss the rule and ask students if they can think of other words that follow the same pattern. Have students complete the Practice section with a partner.

Homework
Have students complete the Academic Words and Phonics practice on *Workbook* pages 14–15.

Lesson 13

Common Core State Standards: RL.3.1, RL.3.3, RL.3.4, RL.3.7, RL.3.10, L.3.4, L.3.4.a, L.3.5.a, L.3.6

Reading 2   *Student Book* pages 26–31
• Use *Transparencies* 3 for Daily Language Practice, Week 3, Day 3.

More About the Big Question Read aloud the Big Question on page 26. Have students think about the question as they read the story. Encourage students to think about how different people are helpful in their community.
Audio Play the audio of the story, stopping to answer questions if students have them. Discuss the general meaning of the story and how it relates to the Big Question.
Reading Strategy Read aloud the bulleted items on page 26. Model the strategy and encourage students to preview and make predictions about the story.
Genre Draw students' attention to the genre label. Tell them that a short story is a story that could be true or not, but it is always only a few pages long.
Read As a class, read the story aloud. Invite students to tell about what they have read, using the pictures as visual aids. Ask them to make predictions based on what they read.
Build Vocabulary Help students recognize how to use the bolded word that is defined on the bottom of page 27.
Key Words Discuss the yellow highlighted words in the story and why they are key words for this reading.
Fluency Activity Complete Fluency Activity 7 in TE on page T30.

Homework
Have students complete the Reader's Companion exercises on *Workbook* page 16

Lesson 14

Common Core State Standards: RL.3.1, RL.3.3, RL.3.4, RL.3.7, RL.3.10, L.3.4, L.3.4.a, L.3.5.a, L.3.6

Reading 2   *Student Book* pages 26–31
• Use *Transparencies* 3 for Daily Language Practice, Week 3, Day 4.
• Have students complete the Reader's Companion on page 17 of the *Workbook*.

Read Have students reread the story silently or listen to the Audio CD.
Reading Strategy Remind students that when they started reading, they made a prediction about what would happen in the story. Tell them that with predictions, there are no right or wrong answers. A prediction is a guess you make based on clues in the text and personal experience.
Respond Have students work in pairs or small groups to complete the Think It Over questions. Discuss the answer to the Analyze question. Encourage students to use the illustrations as evidence to support their opinions.
Fluency Activity Complete Fluency Activity 8 in *TRB* on page 164.

Homework
Have students complete the Comprehension practice on *Workbook* page 18.

Lesson 15

Common Core State Standards: RL.3.1, RL.3.2, SL.3.3, SL.3.6

Learning Strategies *Student Book* pages 32–33

- Use *Transparencies* 3 for Daily Language Practice, Week 3, Day 5.
- Use *Transparencies* 58 and page 144 of the *Teacher's Resource Book* for the Sequence of Events Chart.

More About the Big Question Discuss why each person is important to the community. Ask students to think of other important community members.

Sequence of Events Let students know that the sequence of events is the order in which things happen in a story. Show students how to refer to the text to check the sequence of events. As a class, find the first two events in the Practice activity. When you are sure that students know what to do, have them finish the activity alone or in pairs.

Use a Sequence of Events Chart Copy the Sequence of Events Chart text into the boxes on the transparency. Discuss the order in which things happened in the story. Have students complete the graphic organizer and share their answers.

Apply In pairs, have students retell the story. Encourage students to use the illustrations to help them. Listen for use of key words and vocabulary in their retellings.

Extension You may wish to use extra copies of the Sequence of Events Chart to have students teach each other how to make something.

Homework

Have students complete the Learning Strategies practice on *Workbook* page 19.

Lesson 16

Common Core State Standards: SL.3.1, SL.3.1.c, SL.3.6, L.3.1, L.3.1.d, L.3.1.e

Grammar *Student Book* pages 34–35

- Use *Transparencies* 4 for Daily Language Practice, Week 4, Day 1.
- Have students complete the Unit 1, Reading 2 test in the *Assessments*.

Simple Present Read the introduction and refer to the charts to introduce the different forms of simple present verbs. Have volunteers say a sentence using each form.

Practice Have students work individually. Then have them form small groups and check their answers. Encourage them to refer to the charts on page 34 as they do so.

Apply Have students work in pairs to ask and answer the questions, using simple present tense.

Homework

Have students complete the Grammar and Spelling exercises on *Workbook* pages 20–21.

Lesson 17

Common Core State Standards: W.3.2, W.3.2.a, W.3.4, W.3.5, W.3.10

Writing *Student Book* pages 36–37

- Use *Transparencies* 4 for Daily Language Practice, Week 4, Day 2.
- Use *Transparencies* 58 and page 144 of the *Teacher's Resource Book* for the Sequence of Events Chart.

Describe a Summer Day Read aloud the text at the top of page 36. Refer to the Sequence of Events Chart that you filled in about the story. Read aloud the Writing Prompt. Encourage students to use sensory images when gathering ideas.

Prewrite Give the students copies of the Sequence of Events Chart, or have them copy one into their notebooks. Encourage students to be specific about what they did on a summer day.

Draft Read aloud the sample paragraph to show how to turn the ideas from the Sequence of Events Chart into a paragraph.

Writing Checklist Model how to use the Writing Checklist on page 37 to help you improve the sample paragraph. Encourage students to check for correct use of simple present verbs and the verb *be*. Have students trade papers and do a Peer Review, using the Checklist on page 402.

Homework

Have students prepare a final copy of their paragraph and do the exercises on *Workbook* page 22.

Lesson 18

Common Core State Standards: RL.3.4, SL.3.1, SL.3.1.c, SL.3.6, L.3.4, L.3.4.a, L.3.5.b

Reading 3 Key Words   *Student Book* pages 38–39

- Use *Transparencies* 4 for Daily Language Practice, Week 4, Day 3.
- Use *Transparencies* 39 for Key Words.

Prepare to Read Draw students' attention to the What You Will Learn section. Briefly discuss the topics that will be covered in this reading.

Key Words Read the key words aloud or play them on the Audio CD. Have students repeat each word as it is read aloud.

Words in Context Help students learn the skill of defining words by using context and illustrations to define the highlighted words.

Practice Have students make the flashcards and practice memorizing them with a partner.

Apply Read the text aloud. Have students work in pairs to discuss the question. Circulate and encourage students to use key words in their responses.

Fluency Activity Complete Fluency Activity 9 on TE page T38.

Homework

Have students complete the Key Words practice on *Workbook* page 23.

Lesson 19

Common Core State Standards: RI.3.4, SL.3.1, SL.3.1.c, SL.3.1.d, SL.3.6, L.3.3, L.3.4, L.3.4.a, L.3.4.d

Academic Words & Word Study   *Student Book* pages 40–41

- Use *Transparencies* 4 for Daily Language Practice, Week 4, Day 4.

Academic Words Discuss the definitions of the words and have students listen to the words in context on the Audio CD. Have students complete the Practice activity in their notebooks.

Apply Have students use the academic words when discussing the questions in the Apply section with a partner.

Word Study Read the text at the top of page 41 to illustrate how a dictionary shows the multiple meanings of words. Using a dictionary, show students some other examples of words with more than one meaning. Have students complete the Practice section with a partner.

Homework

Have students complete the Academic Words and Word Study practice on *Workbook* pages 24–25.

Lesson 20

Common Core State Standards: RL.3.1, RL.3.3, RL.3.4, RL.3.7, RL.3.10, L.3.4, L.3.4.a, L.3.5.a, L.3.6

Reading 3 Vocabulary   *Student Book* pages 42–47

- Use *Transparencies* 4 for Daily Language Practice, Week 4, Day 5.

More About the Big Question Read aloud the Big Question on page 42. Have students think about the question as they read the story.
Audio Play the audio of the story, stopping to answer questions if students have them. Discuss the general meaning of the story and how it relates to the Big Question.
Reading Strategy Read aloud the bulleted items on page 42. Model the strategy, telling students how your family may be similar to the one in the story.
Genre Draw students' attention to the genre. Tell students that a personal narrative is a story that is told using the words *I* or *we*.
Read Encourage students to refer to the illustrations as they read.
Build Vocabulary Read the sentences with the highlighted words aloud to the class. Then read each sentence again, replacing the highlighted term with a synonym from the definition.
Check Up Have partners respond to the Check Up questions on pages 43 and 45.
Fluency Activity Do Fluency Activity 10 on TE page T46.

Homework
Have students complete the Think It Over Questions on page 47 in their notebooks.

Lesson 21

Common Core State Standards: RL.3.1, RL.3.3, RL.3.4, RL.3.7, RL.3.10, RI.3.1, RI.3.7, L.3.4, L.3.4.a, L.3.5.a, L.3.6

Reading 3   *Student Book* pages 42–49

- Use *Transparencies* 5 for Daily Language Practice, Week 5, Day 1.
- Have students complete the Comprehension activities on pages 26–27 of the *Workbook*.

Read Students may reread the story silently or listen to the Audio CD.
Reading Strategy After reading the selection, discuss what connections students can make between the family in the story and their own families.
Visual Literacy Draw the students' attention to the photos and captions on pages 48 and 49. Help students understand that these are the girl's family members.
A Closer Look at... Have students make their own family tree. Encourage students to draw pictures of their family members or bring in photographs. Remind students to provide captions with relatives' names and their relationships.
Fluency Activity Complete Fluency Activity 11 in the *TRB* on page 164.

Homework
Have students complete *Workbook* page 28 and ask family members for information to add to their family tree.

Lesson 22

Common Core State Standards: RL.3.1, RL.3.2, SL.3.4, SL.3.6

Learning Strategies   *Student Book* pages 50–51

- Use *Transparencies* 5 for Daily Language Practice, Week 5, Day 2.
- Use *Transparencies* 63 and page 149 of the *Teacher's Resource Book* for the T-Chart.

More About the Big Question Discuss how a family is like a community.
Make Connections Tell students that connections are ways that things are similar.

Encourage students to share ways in which their family's celebrations are like the one in the story.

Practice You may assign the Practice activity as a class discussion, partner activity, or individual written assignment.

Use a T-Chart Copy the T-Chart text into the boxes on the transparency. Discuss what the family in the story does. Have students complete the graphic organizer and share their answers.

Apply In pairs, have students summarize the story. Encourage students to use the illustrations to help them. Listen for use of key words and vocabulary in their retellings.

Extension Have students describe a special family occasion to a partner.

Homework

Have students do the Learning Strategies practice on *Workbook* page 29.

Lesson 23

Common Core State Standards: SL.3.1, SL.3.1.c, SL.3.6, L.3.1, L.3.1.b

Grammar   *Student Book* pages 52–53

• Use *Transparencies* 5 for Daily Language Practice, Week 5, Day 3.
• Have students complete the Unit 1, Reading 3 test in the *Assessments*.

Singular and Plural Nouns Read the introduction and refer to the chart to introduce singular and plural nouns. Have volunteers say a sentence, using each form.

Practice Have students work individually. Then have them form small groups and check their answers. Encourage them to refer to the chart as they do so.

Apply Have students work in pairs to ask and answer the questions, using the correct nouns and articles.

Homework

Have students complete the Grammar and Spelling exercises on *Workbook* pages 30–31.

Lesson 24

Common Core State Standards: W.3.2, W.3.2.a, W.3.4, W.3.5, W.3.10

Writing   *Student Book* pages 54–55

• Use *Transparencies* 5 for Daily Language Practice, Week 5, Day 4.
• Use *Transparencies* 67 and page 153 of the *Teacher's Resource Book* for the Word Web.

Describe a Family Celebration Read aloud the text at the top of page 54. Read aloud the Writing Prompt.

Prewrite Give the students copies of the Word Web, or have them copy the graphic organizer into their notebooks. Encourage students to be specific about who is at the celebration and what they do.

Draft Read the sample paragraph aloud to show how to turn the ideas from the Word Web into a paragraph.

Writing Checklist Model how to use the Writing Checklist on page 55 to help you improve the sample paragraph. Encourage students to check for correct use of nouns and simple present verbs. Have students trade papers and do a Peer Review, using the Checklist on page 402.

Homework

Have students prepare a final copy of their paragraph and do *Workbook* page 32.

Lesson 25

Common Core State Standards: RL.3.10, RI.3.10, W.3.2, W.3.5, W.3.10, SL.3.1, SL.3.1.c, SL.3.1.d, SL.3.6

Apply and Extend *Student Book* pages 56–57
• Use *Transparencies* 5 for Daily Language Practice, Week 5, Day 5.

Link the Readings Have students copy the chart on page 56 into their notebooks and complete it.
Discussion Use the discussion questions to help students review the readings in the unit.
Projects Read aloud the choices for extension projects. Have students begin working on their projects in class.

Homework
Have students finish their projects at home.

Lesson 26

Common Core State Standards: SL.3.1, SL.3.1.c, SL.3.2, SL.3.3, SL.3.4, SL.3.6

Listening & Speaking Workshop,
Writing Workshop   *Student Book* pages 58–62
• Use *Transparencies* 6 for Daily Language Practice, Week 6, Day 1.
• Use *Transparencies* 58 and page 144 of the *Teacher's Resource Book* for the Sequence of Events Chart.

Prepare Read the game's directions and model it aloud. Encourage students to use descriptive words and sensory details to describe a place in the community.
Practice Have students practice reading their descriptions to a partner several times.
Present Allow students to read their descriptions to the class and have their classmates guess what they are describing.
Evaluate Have students answer the reflection questions in their notebooks or with a partner.
Writing Workshop Read the writing prompt aloud and discuss the prewriting sample. Allow students to brainstorm event ideas with a partner and then fill in their own Sequence of Events Chart with writing ideas.

Homework
Have students complete a draft of their event description.

Lesson 27

Common Core State Standards: W.3.2, W.3.2.a, W.3.2.b, W.3.2.c, W.3.2.d, W.3.4, W.3.5, W.3.10

Writing Workshop *Student Book* pages 60–62
• Use *Transparencies* 6 for Daily Language Practice, Week 6, Day 2.

Revise and Edit Read the sample draft aloud. Using the Writing Checklist, see if the class can make the writing more descriptive or find any errors. Encourage students to do this on their own, and then trade papers with a classmate to do a Peer Review. Circulate to give students feedback on their writing.
Project Allow students to share their unit projects with the class.

Homework
Have students create a final copy of their event description.

Lesson 28

Common Core State Standards: W.3.2, W.3.4, W.3.5, W.3.10, RF.3.4, RF.3.4.a, RF.3.4.b, RF.3.4.c

Writing Workshop, Fluency, & Test Review *Student Book* page 81

- Use *Transparencies* 6 for Daily Language Practice, Week 6, Day 3.
- Use *Transparencies* 81 for Unit 1 Big Question to review the Big Questions for the unit.

Writing Workshop Allow students to share their published writing or post it in a central location, where students can read each other's work.

Fluency Have students listen to the sentences on the Audio CD and then practice reading them aloud smoothly.

Practice Working in pairs, have one student read the passage aloud while the other student listens and counts the number of words read in one minute. Have students practice reading the passage several times to improve their reading rate.

Unit 1 Review Using the transparency, focus students' attention on the Big Questions for the unit. Take some time to review the unit's vocabulary, academic words, phonics, word study, and grammar topics to prepare for the Unit Test tomorrow. Have students complete *Workbook* pages 33–34 to review topics in the unit.

Homework
Study for the Unit Test.

Lesson 29

Common Core State Standards: RL.3.1, RL.3.3, RL.3.4, RL.3.7, RI.3.1, RI.3.7

Unit Test *Student Book* pages 2–63

- Use *Transparencies* 6 for Daily Language Practice, Week 6, Day 4.

Test Have students complete the Unit 1 Test in the *Assessments*. Remind students that, if they need to, they can use the *Student Book* to go back and look up the comprehension questions for the readings, but they may not use the book for any other part of the test. Proctor students as they take the test, following the guide in *Assessments*.

Homework
Have students complete the Fluency activities on page 37 of the *Workbook*.

Lesson 30

Common Core State Standards: RL.3.1, RL.3.4, RI.3.1, RI.3.4

Test Preparation *Student Book* pages 64–65

- Use *Transparencies* 6 for Daily Language Practice, Week 6, Day 5.

Taking Tests Draw students' attention to the format being featured in this lesson.
Coaching Corner Guide students through the notes. Use the test sample on the facing page as a reference.
Practice Have students read and complete the test sample independently. Then review the sample with the whole class. Demonstrate how to apply the suggestions provided in the Tips box.

Homework
Have students complete the test preparation practice on *Workbook* pages 39–40.

Lesson 1

Common Core State Standards: RI.3.7, SL.3.1, SL.3.1.c, SL.3.6

Unit Opener   *Student Book* pages 66–67

• Use *Transparencies* 7 for Daily Language Practice, Week 7, Day 1.

Unit: Meeting Challenges Introduce the theme. Explain that a *challenge* is something hard to do. Build students' background on the unit theme by looking at the poster and playing the video.
Fluency Activity Put the Unit 2 Poster on the wall. Do Fluency Activity 1 at the bottom of TE page T66.
The Big Question Read the Big Question aloud. Encourage a discussion of different kinds of challenges and how to meet them.
Listening and Speaking Read the text aloud and ask students to brainstorm words they associate with meeting challenges. Write a list of their words on the board and pronounce them.
Writing Read the text aloud and tell students that they will do this later in the unit.
Quick Write Read the activity aloud, and have students write three sentences. Ask volunteers to share their sentences.

Homework
Ask students to take the Letter Home to their parents, explain it to them, and have their parents sign it.

Lesson 2

Common Core State Standards: RL.3.4, RI.3.4, RI.3.7, W.3.5, W.3.10, SL.3.1, SL.3.1.c, SL.3.6, L.3.4, L.3.4.a, L.3.4.d, L.3.5.b, L.3.6

What do you know about meeting challenges?   *Student Book* pages 68–69

• Use *Transparencies* 7 for Daily Language Practice, Week 7, Day 2.

Words to Know Say each of the terms aloud. Encourage students to point to the correct illustration as they repeat each term with you. Have students work in pairs to do the Practice activity on page 4. Students ask and answer the questions using the new words on the page. Ask students to complete the Write activity independently and share their answer with a partner.
Make Connections Have students work in pairs to complete the activity. Have pairs combine with other pairs to check their answers.
What About You? Have students discuss the question with a partner. Encourage them to use the words they learned on these pages.

Homework
Have students answer the What About You question in their notebooks.

Lesson 3

Common Core State Standards: RI.3.7, SL.3.1, SL.3.1.c, SL.3.6

Kids' Stories from Around the World   *Student Book* pages 70–71

• Use *Transparencies* 7 for Daily Language Practice, Week 7, Day 3.

Kids' Stories from Around the World Read the children's stories. Students can also listen to the peer stories on the Audio CD.

Visual Literacy Draw students' attention to the photographs next to Abebe and Krishna. These photographs show what the children want to do. Have students draw pictures that depict their own challenges. Have them write one sentence that describes their challenge. Create a classroom display titled *Our Challenges.*

What About You? Have students talk about challenges they have faced. Discuss different responses to challenges. Ask students to share ideas about how their experiences are similar to those described in the peer stories.

Fluency Activity Do Fluency Activity 2 at the bottom of TE page T70.

Homework

Have students write a story about themselves, using the peer stories as models.

Lesson 4

Common Core State Standards: RL.3.4, SL.3.1, SL.3.1.c, SL.3.1.d, SL.3.6, L.3.4, L.3.4.a, L.3.5.b

Reading 1 Key Words   *Student Book* pages 72–73
- Use *Transparencies* 7 for Daily Language Practice, Week 7, Day 4.
- Use *Transparencies* 40 for Key Words.

Prepare to Read Draw students' attention to the What You Will Learn section. Briefly discuss the topics that will be covered in this reading.

Key Words Read the key words aloud or play them on the Audio CD. Have students repeat each word as it is read aloud.

Words in Context Have students connect the sentences with the photographs.

Practice Read the text in the *Student Book* and have students complete the activity. Encourage students to use the flashcards as a reference throughout the unit.

Apply Read the text aloud. Have students work in pairs to discuss the question.

Fluency Activity Do Fluency Activity 3 at the bottom of TE page T72.

Homework

Have students complete the Key Words activities on *Workbook* page 41.

Lesson 5

Common Core State Standards: RI.3.4, RF.3.3, SL.3.1, SL.3.1.c, SL.3.6, L.3.4, L.3.4.a

Academic Words & Phonics   *Student Book* pages 74–75
- Use *Transparencies* 7 for Daily Language Practice, Week 7, Day 5.

Academic Words Discuss the definitions of the words and have students listen to the words in context on the Audio CD. Have students complete the Practice activity in their notebooks.

Apply Have students try to use the academic words when discussing the questions in the Apply section with a partner.

Phonics Play the Audio CD to show students the phonics pattern. Discuss the rule and ask students if they can think of other words that follow the same pattern. Have students complete the Practice section with a partner.

Homework

Have students complete the Academic Words and Phonics practice on *Workbook* pages 42–43.

Lesson 6

Common Core State Standards: RL.3.1, RL.3.2, RL.3.3, RL.3.4, RL.3.5, RL.3.7, RL.3.10, L.3.4, L.3.4.a, L.3.5.a, L.3.6

Reading 1   *Student Book* pages 76–79

• Use *Transparencies* 8 for Daily Language Practice, Week 8, Day 1.

More About the Big Question The Big Question for this selection is designed to help students realize that thinking can help them meet a challenge.

Understanding Text Structure Read the list of characters. Review the definitions of *characters* and *narrator.* Discuss how, in a play, the characters tell the story with their words and actions.

Audio Play the audio of the play, stopping to answer questions students may have. Discuss the general meaning of the selection and how it relates to the Big Question.

Reading Strategy Discuss how identifying events in a plot can help a reader better understand a play. Encourage discussion about how Rabbit may get away from Lion.

Read Students can read aloud in groups with one character assigned to each student.

Build Vocabulary Point out that Rabbit and Lion are foes. They are not friends.

Check Up Have students discuss Rabbit's quick thinking in turning the focus away from himself.

Fluency Activity Do Fluency Activity 4 at the bottom of TE page T78.

Homework
Have students complete the Comprehension activities on page 44 of the Workbook.

Lesson 7

Common Core State Standards: RL.3.1, RL.3.2, RL.3.3, RL.3.4, RL.3.5, RL.3.7, RL.3.10, L.3.4, L.3.4.a, L.3.5.a, L.3.6

Reading 1   *Student Book* pages 76–79

• Use *Transparencies* 8 for Daily Language Practice, Week 8, Day 2.
• Have students complete the Reader's Companion on page 45 of the *Workbook*.

Reading Strategy Have students identify five events in the plot. Remind students that they can refer to the illustrations for help.

Reader's Theater Have groups of four act out the play. First, have them decide their roles. Then, have them read the lines to practice. Finally, invite the groups to act out the play in front of the class. Encourage discussion regarding the moral of the story.

Sharing Language and Culture Some students may be familiar with fables or tales from their home cultures that have a moral. Encourage students to share, act out, or bring books of stories that remind them of *The Rabbit and the Lion*.

Respond Have students work in pairs or small groups to complete the Think It Over questions. Discuss the answer to the Analyze question. Encourage students to use the illustrations as evidence to support their opinions.

Fluency Activity Do Fluency Activity 5 on page 164 of the *TRB*.

Homework
Have students complete the Reader's Companion activities on *Workbook* page 46.

Lesson 8

Common Core State Standards: RL.3.1, RL.3.2, SL.3.3, SL.3.6

Learning Strategies   *Student Book* pages 80–81

• Use *Transparencies* 8 for Daily Language Practice, Week 8, Day 3.
• Use *Transparencies* 58 and page 144 of the *Teacher's Resource Book* for the Sequence of Events Chart.

More About the Big Question Discuss how quick thinking helped Rabbit solve his problem and how this strategy can help in other challenging situations.

Events in a Plot Invite a class discussion about how each thing that happens contributes to the story as a whole.

Practice You may assign the Practice activity as a class discussion, partner activity, or individual written assignment. Encourage students to refer to the text to confirm that they have placed events in the correct order.

Use a Sequence of Events Chart Copy the Sequence of Events Chart text into the boxes on the transparency. Discuss how to find the missing events in the play. Have students complete the graphic organizer and share their answers.

Apply In pairs, have students retell the play. Encourage students to use the illustrations to help them. Listen for use of key words and vocabulary in their retellings.

Extension Have pairs of students discuss their skits and prepare to present them to the class.

Homework

Have students do the Learning Strategies practice on *Workbook* page 47.

Lesson 9

Common Core State Standards: SL.3.1, SL.3.1.c, SL.3.6, L.3.1, L.3.1.a, L.3.2, L.3.2.d

Grammar   *Student Book* pages 82–83

• Use *Transparencies* 8 for Daily Language Practice, Week 8, Day 4.
• Have students complete the Unit 2, Reading 1 test in the *Assessments*.

Possessive Nouns and Pronouns Read the introduction and refer to the chart to introduce possessive nouns and pronouns. Have volunteers say a sentence using each form.

Practice Have students work individually. Then have them form small groups and check their answers. Encourage them to refer to the chart as they do so.

Apply Have students work in pairs to ask and answer the questions, using possessive nouns and pronouns.

Homework

Have students complete the Grammar and Spelling exercises on *Workbook* page 48.

Lesson 10

Common Core State Standards: W.3.3, W.3.3.a, W.3.3.b, W.3.4, W.3.5, W.3.10, SL.3.6

Writing   *Student Book* pages 84–85

• Use *Transparencies* 8 for Daily Language Practice, Week 8, Day 5.
• Use *Transparencies* 58 and page 144 of the *Teacher's Resource Book* for the Sequence of Events Chart.

Summarize the Story Brainstorm a list of several stories that students are familiar with. Tell them that a summary tells about the characters and important events in a story.

Prewrite Give the students copies of the Sequence of Events Chart, or have them copy one into their notebooks. Have them write the important events in the correct order.

Draft Model how to turn the information in the graphic organizer into a draft by reading the model paragraph aloud.

Writing Checklist Model how to use the Writing Checklist to help you improve the model paragraph. Encourage students to check for correct use of possessives. Have students trade papers and do a Peer Review, using the Checklist on page 402.

Homework
Have students prepare a final copy of their summaries and do *Workbook* pages 49–50.

Common Core State Standards: RL.3.4, SL.3.1, SL.3.1.c, SL.3.6, L.3.4, L.3.4.a, L.3.5.b

Lesson 11

Reading 2 Key Words   *Student Book* pages 86–87
- Use *Transparencies* 9 for Daily Language Practice, Week 9, Day 1.
- Use *Transparencies* 41 for Key Words.

Prepare to Read Draw students' attention to the What You Will Learn section. Briefly discuss the topics that will be covered in this reading.
Key Words Read the key words aloud or play them on the Audio CD. Have students repeat each word as it is read aloud.
Words in Context Help students learn the skill of defining words by using the context and photos to figure out the meaning of the highlighted words.
Practice Have students make flashcards to help them remember the meaning of the words and give them time to practice using their flashcards with a partner.
Apply Read the text aloud. Have students work in pairs to discuss the questions. Circulate and encourage students to use key words in their responses.
Fluency Activity Do Fluency Activity 6 in TE on page T86.

Homework
Have students complete the Key Words practice on *Workbook* page 51

Common Core State Standards: RI.3.4, RF.3.3, RF.3.3.a, RF.3.3.b, SL.3.1, SL.3.1.c, SL.3.6, L.3.4, L.3.4.a, L.3.4.b

Lesson 12

Academic Words & Word Study   *Student Book* pages 88–89
- Use *Transparencies* 9 for Daily Language Practice, Week 9, Day 2.

Academic Words Discuss the definitions of the words and have students listen to the words in context on the Audio CD. Have students complete the Practice activity in their notebooks.
Apply Have students try to use the academic words when discussing the questions with a partner.
Word Study Play the Audio CD to show students the prefix and suffix. Discuss the meanings and ask students if they can think of other words that follow the same pattern. Have students complete the Practice section with a partner.

Homework
Have students complete the Academic Words and Word Study practice on *Workbook* pages 52–53.

Common Core State Standards: RL.3.1, RL.3.3, RL.3.4, RL.3.7, RL.3.10, L.3.4, L.3.4.a, L.3.5.a, L.3.6

Lesson 13

Reading 2   *Student Book* pages 90–97
- Use *Transparencies* 9 for Daily Language Practice, Week 9, Day 3.

More About the Big Question Read aloud the Big Question on page 90. Have students think about the question as they read the story. Encourage students to think about how strength can help them meet a challenge.

Audio Play the audio of the story, stopping to answer questions if students have them. Discuss the general meaning of the story and how it relates to the Big Question.

Reading Strategy Read aloud the bulleted items on page 90. Model the strategy and encourage students to preview and make predictions about the story.

Genre Draw students' attention to the genre label. Tell them that fables are short stories that teach a lesson.

Read As a class, read aloud the story. Invite students to tell about the visualizations they made while reading. Ask them to make predictions based on what they read.

Key Words Discuss the yellow highlighted words in the story and why they are key words for this reading.

Fluency Activity Complete Fluency Activity 7 in TE on page T96.

Homework
Have students complete the Comprehension activities on *Workbook* page 54.

Lesson 14

Common Core State Standards: RL.3.1, RL.3.3, RL.3.4, RL.3.7, RL.3.10, L.3.4, L.3.4.a, L.3.5.a, L.3.6

Reading 2   *Student Book* pages 90–97
- Use *Transparencies* 9 for Daily Language Practice, Week 9, Day 4.
- Have students complete the Reader's Companion on page 55 of the *Workbook*.

Read Have students reread the story silently or listen to the Audio CD.

Reading Strategy Discuss the illustrations on these pages. Explain that visualizing a story is like seeing a movie in your head. Ask students to try to visualize each event in the story and share some of the pictures they saw in their heads.

Respond Have students work in pairs or small groups to complete the Think It Over questions. Discuss the answer to the Analyze question. Encourage students to use the illustrations as evidence to support their opinions.

Fluency Activity Complete Fluency Activity 8 in *TRB* on page 164.

Homework
Have students complete the Reader's Companion practice on *Workbook* page 56.

Lesson 15

Common Core State Standards: RL.3.1, RL.3.2, RL.3.3, SL.3.6

Learning Strategies   *Student Book* pages 98–99
- Use *Transparencies* 9 for Daily Language Practice, Week 9, Day 5.
- Use *Transparencies* 56 and page 142 of the *Teacher's Resource Book* for the Venn Diagram.

More About the Big Question Discuss how strength can play a role in overcoming challenges and how strength can have different meanings.

Visualizing Students will practice visualizing some of the events in the story. They can also think about how the characters feel. Encourage them to ask themselves: *What do you see? How does it feel? How do the characters feel?* For the Practice activity, have students describe their visualizations to a partner before drawing them.

Use a Compare and Contrast Chart Ask students to think about different types of genres they have read. Briefly review the characteristics of each genre and refer to previous selections. Use the genre summaries for stories, fables, plays, and poems provided on the chart on page T99 in the *Teacher's Edition*.

Apply In pairs, have students retell the fable. Encourage students to use the illustrations to help them. Listen for use of key words and vocabulary in their retellings.

Extension Allow students to act out the story as a play for the rest of the class.

Homework

Have students complete the Learning Strategies practice on *Workbook* page 57.

Lesson 16

Common Core State Standards: SL.3.1, SL.3.1.c, SL.3.6, L.3.1, L.3.1.d, L.3.1.e

Grammar   *Student Book* pages 100–101

• Use *Transparencies* 10 for Daily Language Practice, Week 10, Day 1.
• Have students complete the Unit 2, Reading 2 test in the *Assessments*.

Simple Past: Regular Verbs Read the introduction and refer to the charts to introduce the different forms of regular simple past verbs. Have volunteers say a sentence using each form.

Practice Have students work individually. Then have them form small groups and check their answers. Encourage them to refer to the charts on page 100 as they do so.

Apply Have students work in pairs to ask and answer the questions, using regular simple past verbs.

Homework

Have students complete the Grammar and Spelling exercises on *Workbook* pages 58–59.

Lesson 17

Common Core State Standards: W.3.3, W.3.3.a, W.3.3.b, W.3.4, W.3.5, W.3.10, L.3.1, L.3.1.d, L.3.1.e, SL.3.6

Writing   *Student Book* pages 102–103

• Use *Transparencies* 10 for Daily Language Practice, Week 10, Day 2.
• Use *Transparencies* 63 and page 152 of the *Teacher's Resource Book* for the T-Chart.

Retell a Familiar Story Read aloud the text at the top of page 102. Refer to the Sequence of Events Chart that you completed in the previous Writing lesson. Read aloud the Writing Prompt. Encourage students to use sensory images when gathering ideas.

Prewrite Ask students about stories they know well, and encourage them to briefly retell them to the class. Give the students copies of the T-Chart, or have them copy one into their notebooks.

Draft Read aloud the sample paragraph to show how to turn the ideas from the T-Chart graphic into a paragraph.

Writing Checklist Model how to use the Writing Checklist to help you improve the sample paragraph. Encourage students to check for correct use of simple past verbs. Have students trade papers and do a Peer Review, using the Checklist on page 103.

Homework

Have students prepare a final copy of their paragraph and do the exercises on *Workbook* pages 59–60.

Lesson 18

Common Core State Standards: RI.3.4, SL.3.1, SL.3.1.c, SL.3.6, L.3.4, L.3.4.a, L.3.5.b

Reading 3 Key Words   *Student Book* pages 104–105

- Use *Transparencies* 10 for Daily Language Practice, Week 10, Day 3.
- Use *Transparencies* 42 for Key Words.

Prepare to Read Draw students' attention to the What You Will Learn section. Briefly discuss the topics that will be covered in this reading.

Key Words Read the key words aloud or play them on the Audio CD. Have students repeat each word as it is read aloud.

Words in Context Help students learn the skill of defining words by using context and illustrations to figure out the meaning of the highlighted words.

Practice Have students make the flashcards and practice memorizing them with a partner.

Apply Read the text aloud. Have students work in pairs to discuss the question. Circulate and encourage students to use key words in their responses.

Fluency Activity Complete Fluency Activity 9 on TE page T104.

Homework

Have students complete the Key Words practice on *Workbook* page 61.

Lesson 19

Common Core State Standards: RI.3.4, RF.3.3, SL.3.1, SL.3.1.c, SL.3.6, L.3.3, L.3.4, L.3.4.a

Academic Words & Phonics   *Student Book* pages 106–107

- Use *Transparencies* 10 for Daily Language Practice, Week 10, Day 4.

Academic Words Discuss the definitions of the words and have students listen to the words in context on the Audio CD. Have students complete the Practice activity in their notebooks.

Apply Have students use the academic words when discussing the questions in the Apply section with a partner.

Phonics Read the text at the top of page 107 to show students additional long vowel pairs. Give several sample sentences where students listen for long vowel sounds. Have students complete the Practice section with a partner.

Homework

Have students complete the Academic Words and Phonics practice on *Workbook* pages 62–63.

Lesson 20

Common Core State Standards: RI.3.1, RI.3.2, RI.3.4, RI.3.7, RI.3.10

Reading 3   *Student Book* pages 108–113

- Use *Transparencies* 10 for Daily Language Practice, Week 10, Day 5.

More About the Big Question Read aloud the Big Question on page 108. Have students think about the question as they read the story.

Audio Play the audio of the story, stopping to answer questions if students have them. Discuss the general meaning of the story and how it relates to the Big Question.

Reading Strategy Read aloud the bulleted items on page 108. Model the strategy by having students identify facts and opinions that you model. Illicit from students which words tell them that something is an opinion.

Read Encourage students to refer to the illustrations as they read.

Build Vocabulary Read the sentences with the highlighted words aloud to the class. Then read each sentence again, replacing the highlighted term with a synonym from the definition.

Check Up Have partners respond to the Check Up questions before moving on to the next page.

Fluency Activity Do Fluency Activity 10 on TE page T112.

Homework
Have students complete the Think It Over Questions on page 113 in their notebooks.

Lesson 21

Common Core State Standards: RI.3.1, RI.3.2, RI.3.4, RI.3.7, RI.3.10

Reading 3   *Student Book* pages 108–113
- Use *Transparencies* 11 for Daily Language Practice, Week 11, Day 1.
- Have students complete the Reader's Companion on pages 64–65 of the *Workbook*.

Read Students may reread the story silently or listen to the Audio CD.

Reading Strategy Have students go back through the letter at the end of the story to identify facts and opinions. Discuss the key words in each type of statement. Have students respond to the Reading Strategy questions in their notebooks.

Fluency Activity Complete Fluency Activity 11 in the TRB on page 164.

Homework
Have students complete the Comprehension exercises on *Workbook* page 64.

Lesson 22

Common Core State Standards: RI.3.1, RI.3.3, W.3.2, SL.3.6

Learning Strategies   *Student Book* pages 114–115
- Use *Transparencies* 11 for Daily Language Practice, Week 11, Day 2.
- Use *Transparencies* 67 and page 153 of the *Teacher's Resource Book* for the Word Web.

More About the Big Question After reading the story, have students answer the Big Question. Encourage them to refer to the story to help them.

Practice You may assign the Practice activity as a class discussion, partner activity, or individual written assignment.

Use an Idea Web Have students go back through the story to find two facts and two opinions to put in the web. Then have students share with a partner.

Apply In pairs, have students summarize the story. Encourage students to use the illustrations to help them. Listen for use of key words and vocabulary in their summaries.

Extension Give students the option of starting an actual community project and really mailing their letters to their neighbors.

Homework
Have students do the Learning Strategies practice on *Workbook* page 67.

Lesson 23

Common Core State Standards: SL.3.1, SL.3.1.c, SL.3.6, L.3.1, L.3.1.d, L.3.1.e

Grammar   *Student Book* pages 116–117

- Use *Transparencies* 11 for Daily Language Practice, Week 11, Day 3.
- Have students complete the Unit 2, Reading 3 test in the *Assessments*.

Simple Past: *be* Verbs Read the introduction and refer to the chart to introduce the simple past of *be* verbs. Have volunteers say a sentence using each form.
Practice Have students work individually. Then have them form small groups and check their answers. Encourage them to refer to the chart as they do so.
Apply Have students work in pairs to ask and answer the questions, using the correct form of the verb.

Homework
Have students complete the Grammar and Spelling exercises on *Workbook* pages 68–69.

Lesson 24

Common Core State Standards: W.3.3, W.3.3.a, W.3.4, W.3.5, W.3.10, L.3.3

Writing   *Student Book* pages 118–119

- Use *Transparencies* 11 for Daily Language Practice, Week 11, Day 4.
- Use *Transparencies* 59 and page 145 of the *Teacher's Resource Book* for the Three-Column KWL Chart.

Write a Journal Entry about Your Day Read aloud the text at the top of page 118. Read the Writing Prompt aloud.
Prewrite Give the students copies of the three-column chart, or have them copy one into their notebooks. Have them write about the facts of their day and how they felt about each event. You may wish to model this for students using your own examples.
Draft Read the sample paragraph aloud to show how to turn the ideas from the chart into a paragraph.
Writing Checklist Model how to use the Writing Checklist on page 119 to help you improve the sample paragraph. Encourage students to check for correct use of simple past verbs. Have students trade papers and do a Peer Review using the Checklist on page 402.

Homework
Have students prepare a final copy of their journal entry and do *Workbook* page 70.

Lesson 25

Common Core State Standards: RL.3.9, RL.3.10, RI.3.9, RI.3.10, W.3.2, SL.3.1, SL.3.1.c, SL.3.1.d, SL.3.6

Apply and Extend   *Student Book* pages 120–121

- Use *Transparencies* 11 for Daily Language Practice, Week 11, Day 5.

Link the Readings Discuss the genres of literature and informational text and the characteristics of each. Have students copy the chart on page 120 into their notebooks and complete it. Encourage students to identify the features of each genre to show their answers are correct.
Discussion Use the questions in the Discussion section to help students review the reading selections in the unit and tie them all together.

Projects Read aloud the choices for extension projects. Encourage students to be creative and to choose activities that suit their learning modalities. Have students begin working on their projects in class.

Homework
Have students finish their projects at home.

Lesson 26

Common Core State Standards: SL.3.1, SL.3.1.c, SL.3.2, SL.3.3, SL.3.4, SL.3.6

Listening & Speaking Workshop, *Student Book* pages 122–123
Writing Workshop, *Student Book* page 124
- Use *Transparencies* 12 for Daily Language Practice, Week 12, Day 1.
- Use *Transparencies* 65 and page 152 of the *Teacher's Resource Book* for the Story Map.

Prepare Remind the students how they performed a skit after reading *The Contest* earlier in the unit. Circulate to be sure the groups choose a scene with enough dialogue.
Practice Give groups time to practice performing their skits.
Present Encourage students to use props and visuals in their performances.
Evaluate Have students answer the reflection questions in their notebooks or with a partner.
Writing Workshop Read aloud the writing prompt and discuss personal narratives. Allow students to brainstorm ideas for their stories with a partner and then fill in their own story map with writing ideas.

Homework
Have students complete a draft of their stories.

Lesson 27

Common Core State Standards: W.3.3, W.3.3.a, W.3.3.b, W.3.3.c, W.3.3.d, W.3.4, W.3.5, W.3.10

Writing Workshop *Student Book* pages 124–126
- Use *Transparencies* 12 for Daily Language Practice, Week 12, Day 2.
- Have students complete the writing exercises on *Workbook* page 73.

Revise and Edit Read the sample draft aloud. Using the Writing Checklist, see if the class can make the writing more descriptive or find any errors. Encourage students to do this on their own, and then trade papers with a classmate to do a Peer Review. Circulate to give students feedback on their writing.
Project Allow students to share their unit projects with the class.

Homework
Have students create a final copy of their stories and complete *Workbook* page 74.

Lesson 28

Common Core State Standards: W.3.3, W.3.4, W.3.5, W.3.10, RF.3.4, RF.3.4.a, RF.3.4.b, RF.3.4.c

Writing Workshop, Fluency, & Test Review *Student Book* page 127
- Use *Transparencies* 12 for Daily Language Practice, Week 12, Day 3.
- Use *Transparencies* 82 for Unit 2 Big Question to review the Big Questions for the unit.

Writing Workshop Allow students to share their published writing or post it in a central location where students can read each other's work.

Fluency Have students listen to the sentences on the Audio CD and then practice reading them aloud smoothly.

Practice Working in pairs, have one student read the passage aloud while the other student listens and counts the number of words read in one minute. Circulate to help students identify words in the passage that slowed them down. Have students practice reading the passage several times to improve their reading rate.

Unit 2 Review Using the transparency, focus students' attention on the Big Questions for the unit. Take some time to review the unit's vocabulary, academic words, phonics, word study, and grammar topics to prepare for the Unit Test tomorrow. Have students complete *Workbook* pages 71–72 to review for the test.

Homework
Study for the Unit Test.

Lesson 29

Common Core State Standards: RL.3.1, RL.3.3, RL.3.4, RL.3.7, RI.3.1, RI.3.7

Unit 2 Test   *Student Book* pages 66–127
• Use *Transparencies* 12 for Daily Language Practice, Week 12, Day 4.

Test Have students complete the Unit 2 Test in the *Assessments.* Remind students they can use the *Student Book* to go back and look up the comprehension questions for the readings, but they may not use the book for any other part of the test. Proctor students as they take the test, following the guide in *Assessments.*

Homework
Have students complete the Fluency activities on page 75 of the *Workbook*.

Lesson 30

Common Core State Standards: RL.3.1, RL.3.4, RI.3.1, RI.3.4

Test Preparation   *Student Book* pages 128–129
• Use *Transparencies* 12 for Daily Language Practice, Week 12, Day 5.

Taking Tests Draw students' attention to the test format featured in this lesson.
Coaching Corner Guide students through the notes. Use the test sample on the facing page as a reference.
Practice Have students complete the test sample independently. Review it with the class and demonstrate how to apply the suggestions in the Tips box.

Homework
Have students complete the Test preparation activities on *Workbook* pages 77–78.

Lesson 1

Common Core State Standards: RI.3.7, SL.3.1, SL.3.1.c, SL.3.6

Unit Opener *Student Book* pages 130–131
• Use *Transparencies* 13 for Daily Language Practice, Week 13, Day 1.

Unit: Animals at Home Introduce the theme. Have students call out animals they know as you write them on the board. Have students share what they know about each animal. Build students' background on the unit theme by looking at the poster and playing the video.
Fluency Activity Post the Unit 3 Poster on the wall. Do Fluency Activity 1 at the bottom of TE page T130.
The Big Question Read the Big Question aloud. Explain that people can learn many things about animals, such as what they eat, where they live, and how they grow. Knowing about animals can help us better take care of Earth.
Visual Literacy Have students study the photo of the penguins. SAY *The animals in the photograph are penguins. This photo gives clues about how penguins live. Where do the penguins live? Do you think they live alone or in groups?*
Listening and Speaking Read aloud the text and ask students to brainstorm words that describe where animals live and what animals do. Write a list of their words on the board and pronounce them.
Writing Read the text aloud and tell students that they will do this later in the unit.
Quick Write Read the activity aloud, and have students write three sentences about their favorite animal. Ask volunteers to share their sentences.

Homework
Ask students to take the Letter Home to their parents, explain it to them, and have their parents sign it.

Lesson 2

Common Core State Standards: RL.3.4, RI.3.4, RI.3.7, W.3.5, W.3.10, SL.3.1, SL.3.1.c, SL.3.6, L.3.4, L.3.4.a, L.3.5.b, L.3.4.d, L.3.6

What do you know about Animals?
Student Book pages 132–133
• Use *Transparencies* 13 for Daily Language Practice, Week 13, Day 2.

Words to Know Say each of the terms aloud. Encourage students to point to the correct illustration as they repeat each term with you. Direct students' attention to the Practice activity. Have students work in pairs and complete the sentence stem with the words provided. Ask students to complete the Write activity independently and share their answer with a partner.
Make Connections Have students work in pairs to complete the activity. Have pairs combine with other pairs to check their answers.
What About You? Have students discuss the question with a partner. Encourage them to use the words they learned on these pages.

Homework
Have students answer the What About You question in their notebooks.

Lesson 3

Common Core State Standards: RI.3.7, SL.3.1, SL.3.1.c, SL.3.6

Kids' Stories from Around the World *Student Book* pages 134–135
• Use *Transparencies* 13 for Daily Language Practice, Week 13, Day 3.

Kids' Stories from Around the World Read the children's stories. Students can also listen to the peer stories on the Audio CD.

Visual Literacy Use the stories to elicit prior knowledge, generate discussion, and help students tell their own stories about animals.

What About You? Ask students to think about visits they have made with friends, family, and their class to wildlife centers, national parks, or zoos. Invite students to share what they know about national parks in the United States or in other countries.

Fluency Activity Do Fluency Activity 2 at the bottom of TE page T134.

Homework

Have students find a nonfiction library book about an animal.

Lesson 4

Common Core State Standards: RL.3.4, SL.3.1, SL.3.1.c, SL.3.6, L.3.4, L.3.4.a, L.3.5.b

Reading 1 Key Words   *Student Book* pages 136–137

- Use *Transparencies* 13 for Daily Language Practice, Week 13, Day 4.
- Use *Transparencies* 43 for Key Words.

Prepare to Read Draw students' attention to the What You Will Learn section. Briefly discuss the topics that will be covered in this reading.

Key Words Read the key words aloud or play them on the Audio CD. Have students repeat each word as it is read aloud.

Words in Context Have students connect the sentences with the photographs.

Practice Model how to make a three-column page for vocabulary in their notebooks. Encourage students to use the page as a reference throughout the unit.

Apply Read the text aloud. Have students work in pairs to discuss the question.

Fluency Activity Do Fluency Activity 3 at the bottom of TE page T136.

Homework

Have students complete the Key Words activities on *Workbook* page 79.

Lesson 5

Common Core State Standards: RI.3.4, RF.3.3, SL.3.1, SL.3.1.c, SL.3.6, L.3.4, L.3.4.a

Academic Words & Phonics   *Student Book* pages 138–139

- Use *Transparencies* 13 for Daily Language Practice, Week 13, Day 5.

Academic Words Discuss the definitions of the words and have students listen to the words in context on the Audio CD. Have students complete the Practice activity in their notebooks.

Apply Have students try to use the academic words when discussing the questions with a partner.

Phonics Play the Audio CD to show students the phonics pattern. Discuss the consonant clusters and ask students if they can think of other words that follow the same pattern. Have students complete the Practice section with a partner. Encourage students to look through this and other units and list words that begin with *r*-blends, *s*-blends, or *l*-blends.

Homework

Have students complete the Academic Words and Phonics practice on *Workbook* pages 80–81.

Lesson 6

Common Core State Standards: RL.3.1, RL.3.4, RL.3.7, RL.3.10, RI.3.1, RI.3.7, L.3.4, L.3.4.a, L.3.5.a, L.3.6

Reading 1 *Student Book* pages 140–143

• Use *Transparencies* 14 for Daily Language Practice, Week 14, Day 1.

More About the Big Question To help students relate the Big Question to their own lives, have students think about their homes. Ask them why their home is important to them. Ask why an animal's home might be important to it.

Understanding Text Structure Remind students about the genre of poetry and how it looks and sounds different from a narrative. Point out that many poems have rhyming words. Give some examples of words that rhyme and ask students to listen for this feature in the poem.

Audio Play the audio of the poem, stopping to answer questions students may have. Discuss the general meaning of the selection and how it relates to the Big Question.

Reading Strategy Help students understand that they make inferences when they figure out something that is not directly stated in the selection. SAY *In the poem, I learned about many different animal habitats. They can live in hot places, in dry places, and even underground. I made the inference that animals can live almost anywhere.*

Read Have students take turns reading aloud the stanzas of the poem.

Fluency Activity Do Fluency Activity 5 on page 164 of the TRB.

Homework

Have students complete the Comprehension activities on page 82 of the *Workbook*.

Lesson 7

Common Core State Standards: RL.3.1, RL.3.4, RL.3.7, RL.3.10, RI.3.1, RI.3.7, W.3.8, L.3.4, L.3.4.a, L.3.5.a, L.3

Reading 1 *Student Book* pages 140–145

• Use *Transparencies* 14 for Daily Language Practice, Week 14, Day 2.
• Have students complete the Reader's Companion on page 83 of the *Workbook*.

Read Have students read the poem aloud or follow along on the Audio CD.

Respond Have students work in pairs or small groups to complete the Think It Over questions. Discuss the answer to the Analyze question. Encourage students to use the illustrations as evidence to support their opinions.

A Closer Look at… Draw students' attention to the photographs and captions on pages 144–145. Guide them to recognize that each photograph has a corresponding label and a caption. Have volunteers read aloud the captions as students follow along in their books. Then discuss the photographs and the text.

Activity to Do Ask students to select another animal to research using the Internet, reference books, or science magazines. SAY *Choose pictures and write captions that describe the animal and its habitat. What does the animal look like? What is the animal's habitat like? What does the animal eat?*

Fluency Activity Do Fluency Activity 4 at the bottom of TE page T142.

Homework

Have students complete the Reader's Companion activities on *Workbook* page 84 and bring in pictures of the animal they chose.

Lesson 8

Common Core State Standards: RL.3.1, RL.3.2, RL.3.5, W.3.8, SL.3.4, SL.3.6

Learning Strategies *Student Book* pages 146–147

- Use *Transparencies* 14 for Daily Language Practice, Week 14, Day 3.
- Use *Transparencies* 59 and page 145 of the *Teacher's Resource Book* for the KWL Chart.

More About the Big Question Discuss how important students' homes are and how important animal habitats are to both animals and people.

Inferences Remind students that to make an inference, readers use what they read and what they already know to figure out something that is not directly stated. Prompt students to make inferences about the poem by asking, *What do you know? What do you want to know? What did you learn?*

Practice You may assign the Practice activity as a class discussion, partner activity, or individual written assignment.

Use a KWL Chart Have students write: **K** one thing they knew about animals and where they live before reading the selection; **W** one thing they wanted to learn about animals from the poem; **L** one thing they learned about animals from the poem. Have students complete the graphic organizer and share their answers.

Apply In pairs, have students summarize the poem. Encourage students to use the illustrations to help them. Listen for use of key words and vocabulary in their summaries.

Extension Have students complete the extension activity about a new animal and share it with the class.

Homework

Have students do the Learning Strategies practice on *Workbook* page 85.

Lesson 9

Common Core State Standards: SL.3.1, SL.3.1.c, SL.3.6, L.3.1

Grammar *Student Book* pages 148–149

- Use *Transparencies* 14 for Daily Language Practice, Week 14, Day 4.
- Have students complete the Unit 3, Reading 1 test in the *Assessments*.

Prepositions and Prepositional Phrases Read the introduction and refer to the chart to introduce the prepositions and prepositional phrases. Have volunteers say a sentence, using each one.

Practice Have students work individually. Then have them form small groups and check their answers. Encourage them to refer to the chart as they do so.

Apply Have students work in pairs to ask and answer the questions, using different prepositional phrases.

Homework

Have students complete the Grammar and Spelling exercises on *Workbook* pages 86–87.

Lesson 10

Common Core State Standards: W.3.4, W.3.5, W.3.10, SL.3.6

Writing *Student Book* pages 150–151

- Use *Transparencies* 14 for Daily Language Practice, Week 14, Day 5.

Write a Poem Brainstorm a list of animals that students know about.

Prewrite Draw a chart like the one on page 150 on the board and have students copy it into their notebooks. Have them record their ideas in the chart.

Draft Model how to turn the information in the chart into a poem by reading aloud the sample.

Writing Checklist Model how to use the Writing Checklist to help you improve the sample. Encourage students to check for correct use of prepositions and prepositional phrases. Have students trade papers and do a Peer Review using the Checklist on page 402.

Homework

Have students prepare a final copy of their poem and do *Workbook* page 88.

Lesson 11

Common Core State Standards: RI.3.4, RI.3.7, SL.3.1, SL.3.1.c, SL.3.6, L.3.4, L.3.4.a, L.3.5.b

Reading 2 Key Words   *Student Book* pages 152–153

- Use *Transparencies* 15 for Daily Language Practice, Week 15, Day 1.
- Use *Transparencies* 44 for Key Words.

Prepare to Read Draw students' attention to the What You Will Learn section. Briefly discuss the topics that will be covered in this reading.

Key Words Read the key words aloud or play them on the Audio CD. Have students repeat each word as it is read aloud.

Words in Context Help students learn the skill of defining words by using the context and photos to figure out the meaning of the highlighted words.

Practice Have students make flashcards to help them remember the meaning of the words and give them time to practice using their flashcards with a partner.

Apply Read the text aloud. Have students work in pairs to discuss the question. Circulate and encourage students to use key words in their responses.

Fluency Activity Do Fluency Activity 6 in the TE on page T152.

Homework

Have students complete the Key Words practice on *Workbook* page 89.

Lesson 12

Common Core State Standards: RI.3.4, SL.3.1, SL.3.1.c, SL.3.6, L.3.4, L.3.4.a

Academic Words & Word Study   *Student Book* pages 154–155

- Use *Transparencies* 15 for Daily Language Practice, Week 15, Day 2.

Academic Words Discuss the definitions of the words and have students listen to the words in context on the Audio CD. Have students complete the Practice activity in their notebooks.

Apply Have students try to use the academic words when discussing the questions with a partner.

Word Study Play the Audio CD to show students about compound nouns. Discuss the meanings and ask students if they can think of other words that follow the same pattern. Have students complete the Practice section with a partner.

Homework

Have students complete the Academic Words and Word Study practice on *Workbook* pages 90–91.

Lesson 13

Common Core State Standards: RI.3.1, RI.3.2, RI.3.3, RI.3.4, RI.3.7, RI.3.8, RI.3.10

Reading 2   *Student Book* pages 156–159
- Use *Transparencies* 15 for Daily Language Practice, Week 15, Day 3.

More About the Big Question Read aloud the Big Question on page 156. Have students think about the question as they read the story. Encourage students to think about how camouflage helps animals.

Audio Play the audio of the story, stopping to answer questions if students have them. Discuss the general meaning of the story and how it relates to the Big Question.

Reading Strategy Read aloud the bulleted items on page 156. Model the strategy and have students look for cause and effect as they read.

Genre Draw students' attention to the genre label. Tell them that a photo essay uses photos to help explain the information in the text.

Read Have volunteers read the introductory paragraphs on pages 156–157 aloud. Then have students look at each photo and read the caption. Discuss how each photo helps explain the information in the introductory paragraphs.

Key Words Discuss the yellow highlighted words in the story and why they are key words for this reading.

Fluency Activity Complete Fluency Activity 7 in the TE on page T158.

Homework
Have students complete the Comprehension activities exercises on *Workbook* page 92.

Lesson 14

Common Core State Standards: RI.3.1, RI.3.2, RI.3.3, RI.3.4, RI.3.7, RI.3.8, RI.3.10

Reading 2   *Student Book* pages 156–159
- Use *Transparencies* 15 for Daily Language Practice, Week 15, Day 4.
- Have students complete the Reader's Companion on page 93 of the *Workbook*.

Read Have students reread the story silently or listen to the Audio CD and follow along.

Reading Strategy Have students work in small groups to respond to the Reading Strategy questions on page 159.

Respond Have students work in pairs or small groups to complete the Think It Over questions. Discuss the answer to the Analyze question. Encourage students to use the illustrations as evidence to support their opinions.

Fluency Activity Complete Fluency Activity 8 in the TRB on page 164.

Homework
Have students complete the Reader's Companion on *Workbook* page 94.

Lesson 15

Common Core State Standards: RI.3.1, RI.3.12, RI.3.8, SL.3.6

Learning Strategies   *Student Book* pages 160–161
- Use *Transparencies* 15 for Daily Language Practice, Week 15, Day 5.
- Use *Transparencies* 62 and page 148 of the *Teacher's Resource Book* for the Cause and Effect Chart.

More About the Big Question Discuss how an animal's camouflage makes its habitat more important.

Cause and Effect Prompt students to identify cause and effect as they summarize. Ask: *What is one cause? What is one effect of that cause?* Have students complete the Practice activity independently or in pairs.

Use a Cause and Effect Chart Copy the chart on the board. Encourage students to suggest responses to fill in the causes and effects. Let students know they can refer to the selection to find details.

Apply In pairs, have students summarize the selection to a partner. Encourage students to use the illustrations to help them. Listen for use of key words and vocabulary in their summaries.

Extension Have students share their drawings with the class and explain how their features help them blend in with their surroundings.

Homework
Have students complete the Learning Strategies practice on *Workbook* page 95.

Lesson 16

Common Core State Standards: SL.3.1, SL.3.1.c, SL.3.6, L.3.1, L.3.1.a, L.3.1.g

Grammar   *Student Book* pages 162–163
- Use *Transparencies* 16 for Daily Language Practice, Week 16, Day 1.
- Have students complete the Unit 3, Reading 2 test in the *Assessments*.

Adjectives and Adverbs Read the introduction and refer to the charts to introduce these descriptive words. Have volunteers say a sentence using each one.

Practice Have students work individually. Then have them form small groups and check their answers. Encourage them to refer to the charts on page 162 as they do so.

Apply Have students work in pairs to ask and answer the questions, using adjectives and adverbs.

Homework
Have students complete the Grammar and Spelling exercises on *Workbook* pages 96–97.

Lesson 17

Common Core State Standards: W.3.3, W.3.3.a, W.3.4, W.3.5, W.3.10

Writing   *Student Book* pages 164–165
- Use *Transparencies* 16 for Daily Language Practice, Week 16, Day 2.
- Use *Transparencies* 58 and page 144 of the *Teacher's Resource Book* for the Sequence of Events Chart.

Write a Friendly Letter Read the sample friendly letter aloud. Review the different parts of a letter.

Prewrite Ask students to think about the animals they read about in the selection. Give the students copies of the Sequence of Events Chart, or have them copy one into their notebooks.

Draft Read the sample letter aloud to show students how to turn the ideas from the chart into their own friendly letter.

Writing Checklist Model how to use the Writing Checklist to help you improve the sample letter. Encourage students to check for correct use of the parts of a letter. Have students trade papers and do a Peer Review, using the Checklist on page 402.

Homework
Have students prepare a final copy of their letter and do the exercises on *Workbook* page 98.

Lesson 18

Common Core State Standards: RI.3.4, RI.3.7, SL.3.1, SL.3.1.c, SL.3.6, L.3.4, L.3.4.a, L.3.5.b

Reading 3 Key Words   *Student Book* pages 166–167
- Use *Transparencies* 16 for Daily Language Practice, Week 16, Day 3.
- Use *Transparencies* 45 for Key Words.

Prepare to Read Draw students' attention to the What You Will Learn section. Briefly discuss the topics that will be covered in this reading.
Key Words Read the key words aloud or play them on the Audio CD. Have students repeat each word as it is read aloud.
Words in Context Help students learn the skill of defining words by using context and illustrations to figure out the meaning of the highlighted words.
Practice Have students draw pictures of the key words and label the each picture with a sentence.
Apply Read the text aloud. Have students work in pairs to discuss the questions. Circulate and encourage students to use key words in their responses.
Fluency Activity Complete Fluency Activity 9 in the TE on page T166.

Homework
Have students complete the Key Words practice on *Workbook* page 99.

Lesson 19

Common Core State Standards: RI.3.4, RF.3.3, SL.3.1, SL.3.1.c, SL.3.6, L.3.3, L.3.4, L.3.4.a

Academic Words & Phonics   *Student Book* pages 168–169
- Use *Transparencies* 16 for Daily Language Practice, Week 16, Day 4.

Academic Words Discuss the definitions of the words and have students listen to the words in context on the Audio CD. Have students complete the Practice activity in their notebooks.
Apply Have students try to use the academic words when discussing the questions with a partner.
Phonics Read the text at the top of page 169 to introduce the concept of a consonant digraph. Give several sample sentences where students listen for consonant digraphs. Have students complete the Practice section with a partner.

Homework
Have students complete the Academic Words and Phonics practice on *Workbook* pages 100–101.

Lesson 20

Common Core State Standards: RI.3.1, RI.3.2, RI.3.3, RI.3.4, RI.3.7, RI.3.8, RI.3.10

Reading 3 *Student Book* pages 170–173

• Use *Transparencies* 16 for Daily Language Practice, Week 16, Day 5.

More About the Big Question Read aloud the Big Question on page 170. Have students think about how animals are important to people.

Audio Play the audio of the story, stopping to answer questions if students have them. Discuss the general meaning of the story and how it relates to the Big Question.

Reading Strategy Read aloud the bulleted items on page 170. Discuss with students how identifying the steps in a process can help them to better understand how information is connected.

Genre Draw students' attention to the genre. Point out that informational text is nonfiction because it tells about something that is true.

Read Encourage students to refer to the illustrations as they read the story aloud.

Build Vocabulary Read the sentences with the highlighted words aloud to the class. Then read each sentence again, replacing the highlighted term with a synonym from the definition.

Before You Go On Have partners respond to the Check Up question on page 171 .

Fluency Activity Do Fluency Activity 10 in the TE on page T172.

Homework

Have students complete the Think It Over Questions on page 173 in their notebooks.

Lesson 21

Common Core State Standards: RI.3.1, RI.3.2, RI.3.3, RI.3.4, RI.3.7, RI.3.8, RI.3.10

Reading 3 *Student Book* pages 170–173

• Use *Transparencies* 17 for Daily Language Practice, Week 17, Day 1.
• Have students complete the Comprehension activities on page 102 of the *Workbook*.

Read Students may reread the story silently or listen to the Audio CD.

Reading Strategy Have groups respond to the Reading Strategy questions on page 173 and share their responses with the class. Remind students to pay attention to the order of the steps in a process.

Respond Have students respond to the Think It Over questions in their notebooks. As a class, discuss the Analyze question. Encourage students to find evidence in the text to support their answer.

Fluency Activity Complete Fluency Activity 11 in the TRB on page 164.

Homework

Have students complete the Reader's Companion on *Workbook* pages 103–104.

Lesson 22

Common Core State Standards: RI.3.1, RI.3.3, RI.3.8, SL.3.6

Learning Strategies *Student Book* pages 174–175

• Use *Transparencies* 17 for Daily Language Practice, Week 17, Day 2.
• Use *Transparencies* 58 and page 144 of the *Teacher's Resource Book* for the Sequence of Events Chart.

More About the Big Question Invite a discussion about how animal changes are important to people.

Copyright © by Pearson Education, Inc.

Steps in a Process Authors use sequence words such as *first, then, next,* and *last; first, second, third,* and *fourth;* or numbers to tell the reader they are showing a sequence of events. Tell students that when they see these clue words, they should look closely to see if the author is presenting a sequence of events or steps in a process. Students can put the steps in a frog's life in their natural order. Prompt students with questions such as *What happens first?* or *What happens next?*

Practice You may assign the Practice activity as a class discussion, partner activity, or individual written assignment.

Use a Sequence of Events Chart Discuss the butterfly life cycle in the sample chart. Encourage students to refer to the selection to verify their answers.

Extension Give students their own copies of the Sequence of Events Chart to show the steps of something they can do. Allow them to share their charts with the class.

Homework
Have students do the Learning Strategies practice on *Workbook* page 105.

Lesson 23

Common Core State Standards: SL.3.1, SL.3.1.c, SL.3.6, L.3.1, L.3.1.a, L.3.1.g

Grammar   *Student Book* pages 176–177

- Use *Transparencies* 17 for Daily Language Practice, Week 17, Day 3.
- Have students complete the Unit 3, Reading 3 test in the *Assessments*.

Adverbs of Time Read the introduction and refer to the chart to introduce the adverbs of time. Have volunteers say a sentence using one.

Practice Have students work individually. Then have them form small groups and check their answers. Encourage them to refer to the chart as they do so.

Apply Have students work in pairs to ask and answer the question, using the correct adverbs.

Homework
Have students complete the Grammar and Spelling exercises on *Workbook* pages 106–107.

Lesson 24

Common Core State Standards: W.3.3, W.3.3a, W.3.3.b, W.3.3.c, W.3.4, W.3.5, W.3.10

Writing   *Student Book* pages 178–179

- Use *Transparencies* 17 for Daily Language Practice, Week 17, Day 4.
- Use *Transparencies* 55 and page 141 of the *Teacher's Resource Book* for the Main Idea/Supporting Details Chart.

Write a Personal Narrative Read aloud the text at the top of page 178. Read the Writing Prompt aloud. Brainstorm about the types of events students can write about.

Prewrite Give the students copies of the Main Idea/Supporting Details Chart, or have them copy one into their notebooks. Remind students to use sensory details, and use adverbs of time correctly.

Draft Read aloud the sample paragraph to show how to turn the ideas from the chart into a story.

Writing Checklist Model how to use the Writing Checklist on page 179 to help you improve the sample. Encourage students to check for correct use of adjectives, adverbs, and prepositions. Have students trade papers and do a Peer Review using the Checklist on page 408.

Homework
Have students prepare a final copy of their stories and do *Workbook* page 108.

Lesson 25

Common Core State Standards: RL.3.9, RL.3.10, RI.3.9, RI.3.10, W.3.2, W.3.3, SL.3.1, SL.3.1.c, SL.3.1.d, SL.3.4, SL.3.6

Apply and Extend *Student Book* **pages 180–181**
• Use *Transparencies* 17 for Daily Language Practice, Week 17, Day 5.

Link the Readings Discuss the genres of literature and informational text and the characteristics of each. Have students copy the chart on page 180 into their notebooks and complete it. Encourage students to identify the features of each genre.
Discussion Use the discussion questions to help students review the reading selections from the unit and to tie them all together with the Big Question.
Projects Read aloud the choices. Encourage students to be creative and to choose activities that suit their modalities. Have students begin their projects in class.

Homework
Have students finish their projects at home.

Lesson 26

Common Core State Standards: SL.3.1, SL.3.1.c, SL.3.2, SL.3.3, SL.3.6

Listening & Speaking Workshop, *Student Book* **pages 182–183**
Writing Workshop, Student Book page 184
• Use *Transparencies* 18 for Daily Language Practice, Week 18, Day 1.
• Use *Transparencies* 65 and page 151 of the *Teacher's Resource Book* for the Story Map.

Prepare Remind the students how they have recited poems in earlier units. Discuss how poetry has rhythm and, sometimes, rhyme. Encourage them to use these devices when writing their own poems.
Practice Give students time to practice reciting their poems.
Present Allow students to have a copy of the poem on hand, just in case they forget a word while presenting.
Evaluate Have students answer the reflection questions in their notebooks or with a partner.
Writing Workshop Read aloud the writing prompt and discuss the prewriting sample. Allow students to brainstorm ideas for their stories with a partner and then fill in their own Story Map with writing ideas.

Homework
Have students complete a draft of their stories.

Lesson 27

Common Core State Standards: W.3.3, W.3.3a, W.3.3.b, W.3.3.c, W.3.3.d, W.3.4, W.3.5, W.3.10

Writing Workshop *Student Book* **pages 184–185**
• Use *Transparencies* 18 for Daily Language Practice, Week 18, Day 2.
• Have students complete the writing exercises on *Workbook* page 111.

Revise and Edit Read the sample draft aloud. Using the Writing Checklist, see if the class can make the writing more descriptive or find any errors. Encourage students to do this on their own, and then trade papers with a classmate to do a Peer Review.

Project Allow students to share their unit projects with the class.

Homework
Have students create a final copy of their stories and complete *Workbook* page 112.

Lesson 28

Common Core State Standards: RL.3.1, RL.3.3, RL.3.4, RL.3.7, RI.3.1, RI.3.7

Writing Workshop, Fluency & Test Review   *Student Book* page 187
• Use *Transparencies* 18 for Daily Language Practice, Week 18, Day 3.
• Use *Transparencies* 83 for Unit 3 Big Question to review the Big Questions for the unit.

Writing Workshop Allow students to share their published writing.
Fluency Point out that you can practice fluency by reading a passage over and over until you read it smoothly. Have students listen to the sentences on the Audio CD and then practice reading them aloud smoothly.
Practice Working in pairs, have one student read the passage aloud while the other student listens and counts the number of words read in one minute. Circulate to help students identify words in the passage that slowed them down. Have students practice reading the passage several times to improve their reading rate.
Unit 3 Review Using the transparency, focus on the Big Questions for the unit. Review the unit's vocabulary, academic words, phonics, word study, and grammar topics to prepare for the Unit Test tomorrow. Have students complete *Workbook* pages 109–110.

Homework
Study for the Unit Test.

Lesson 29

Common Core State Standards: RI.3.1, RI.3.2, RI.3.23, RI.3.4

Unit 3 Test   *Student Book* pages 130–187
• Use *Transparencies* 18 for Daily Language Practice, Week 18, Day 4.

Test Have students complete the Unit 3 Test in the *Assessments*. Remind students that they can use the *Student Book* to go back and look up only the comprehension questions for the readings. Proctor students as they take the test, following the guide in *Assessments*.

Homework
Have students complete the Fluency activities on page 113 of the *Workbook*.

Lesson 30

Common Core State Standards: RL.3.1, RL.3.4, RI.3.1, RI.3.4

Test Preparation   *Student Book* pages 188–189
• Use *Transparencies* 18 for Daily Language Practice, Week 18, Day 5.

Taking Tests Draw students' attention to the test format featured in this lesson.
Coaching Corner Guide students through the notes. Use the test sample on the facing page as a reference.
Practice Have students complete the test sample independently. Review it with the class and demonstrate how to apply the suggestions in the Tips box.

Homework
Have students complete the test preparation on *Workbook* pages 115–116.

Lesson 1
Common Core State Standards: RI.3.7, SL.3.1, SL.3.1.c, SL.3.6

Unit Opener *Student Book* pages 190–191
• Use *Transparencies* 19 for Daily Language Practice, Week 19, Day 1.

Unit: Great Ideas Introduce the theme. Have students work in pairs to brainstorm great ideas they or other people may have had. Then ask one student per group to share two ideas with the class. Build students' background on the unit theme by looking at the poster and playing the video.

Fluency Activity Put the Unit 4 Poster on the wall. Do Fluency Activity 1 at the bottom of TE page T190.

The Big Question Read the Big Question aloud. Ask students to share some great ideas that have made the world a better place.

Listening and Speaking Read aloud the text in the box. Explain that inventions are tools, machines, or even ways of doing things that come from great ideas.

Writing Read the text aloud and tell students that they will do this later in the unit.

Quick Write Read the activity aloud, and have students list at least three other areas in which people can have great ideas. Have volunteers share their responses and write them on a chart that you can refer to later in the unit.

Homework
Ask students to take the Letter Home to their parents, explain it to them, and have their parents sign it.

Lesson 2
Common Core State Standards: RL.3.4, RI.3.4, RI.3.7, W.3.5, W.3.10, SL.3.1, SL.3.1.c, SL.3.6, L.3.4, L.3.4.a, L.3.5.b, L.3.4.d, L.3.6

What do you know about great ideas? *Student Book* pages 192–193
• Use *Transparencies* 19 for Daily Language Practice, Week 19, Day 2.

Words to Know Say each of the terms aloud. Encourage students to point to the correct illustration as they repeat each term with you. Direct students' attention to the Practice activity. Have students work in pairs and complete the sentence stem with the words provided. Ask students to complete the Write activity independently and share their answer with a partner.

Make Connections Have students work in pairs to complete the activity. Have pairs combine with other pairs to check their answers.

What About You? Have students discuss the question with a partner. Encourage them to use the words they learned on these pages.

Homework
Have students answer the What About You question in their notebooks.

Lesson 3
Common Core State Standards: RI.3.7, SL.3.1, SL.3.1.c, SL.3.6

Kids' Stories from Around the World *Student Book* pages 194–195
• Use *Transparencies* 19 for Daily Language Practice, Week 19, Day 3.

Kids' Stories from Around the World Read the children's stories. Students can also listen to the peer stories on the Audio CD.

Visual Literacy Have students follow the lines from the photographs on the page to the locations on the map. Say the names of each location and have students repeat the locations aloud.

What About You? Students can either share great ideas they have had or those they have heard About or witnessed. Have students compare their own stories to the stories of the children in these pages. Guide them to recognize some of fundamental similarities that may exist, such as how all the great ideas benefited people.

Fluency Activity Do Fluency Activity 2 at the bottom of TE page T194.

Homework
Have students write about an idea they think is great.

Lesson 4

Common Core State Standards: RI.3.4, SL.3.1, SL.3.1.c, SL.3.6, L.3.4, L.3.4.a, L.3.5.b

Reading 1 Key Words   *Student Book* pages 196–197
- Use *Transparencies* 19 for Daily Language Practice, Week 19, Day 4.
- Use *Transparencies* 46 for Key Words.

Prepare to Read Draw students' attention to the What You Will Learn section. Briefly discuss the topics that will be covered in this reading.

Key Words Read the key words aloud or play them on the Audio CD. Have students repeat each word as it is read aloud. Ask students what the words mean after they hear the sentences.

Words in Context Have students connect the sentences with the photographs.

Practice Have students make flashcards for the key words. Allow students to practice using the flashcards with a partner.

Apply Read the text aloud. Have students work in pairs to discuss the question. Encourage them to use key words in their answers.

Fluency Activity Do Fluency Activity 3 at the bottom of TE page T196.

Homework
Have students complete the Key Words activities on *Workbook* page 117.

Lesson 5

Common Core State Standards: RI.3.4, RF.3.3, RF.3.3.a, SL.3.1, SL.3.1.c, SL.3.6, L.3.4, L.3.4.a

Academic Words & Word Study   *Student Book* pages 198–199
- Use *Transparencies* 19 for Daily Language Practice, Week 19, Day 5.

Academic Words Discuss the definitions of the words and have students listen to the words in context on the Audio CD. Have students complete the Practice activity in their notebooks.

Apply Have students try to use the academic words when discussing the questions in the Apply section with a partner.

Word Study Play the Audio CD to show students the pronunciation of -*ed.* Discuss how -*ed* endings indicate that something happened in the past and ask students if they can think of other words that follow the same pattern. Have students complete the Practice section with a partner. Encourage students to look through this and other units and list words that follow this pattern.

Homework
Have students complete the Academic Words and Word Study practice on *Workbook* pages 118–119.

Lesson 6

Common Core State Standards: RI.3.1, RI.3.2, RI.3.3, RI.3.4, RI.3.7, RI.3.8, RI.3.10

Reading 1   *Student Book* pages 200–205
• Use *Transparencies* 20 for Daily Language Practice, Week 20, Day 1.

More About the Big Question Discuss how people use great ideas to help others.
Understanding Text Structure Draw students' attention to the genre. Have students name magazines they or their family members read. Use students' responses to explain that magazines provide information about topics readers are interested in.
Audio Play the audio of the article, stopping to answer questions students may have. Discuss the general meaning of the selection and how it relates to the Big Question.
Reading Strategy Explain that sometimes readers may have to make inferences about the problems and solutions based on what they read and what they know. Use the questions on page T205 of the *Teacher's Edition* to elicit discussion about the problems and solutions in the reading.
Read Have volunteers read the article aloud. Remind them to read the subheads and captions, too. Other students can respond to the Before You Go On questions.
Fluency Activity Do Fluency Activity 4 at the bottom of TE page T204.

Homework
Have students complete the Comprehension activities on page 120 of the *Workbook*.

Lesson 7

Common Core State Standards: RI.3.1, RI.3.2, RI.3.3, RI.3.4, RI.3.7, RI.3.8, RI.3.10, W.3.8

Reading 1   *Student Book* pages 200–207
• Use *Transparencies* 20 for Daily Language Practice, Week 20, Day 2.
• Have students begin the Reader's Companion on page 121 of the *Workbook*.

Read Have students read the article aloud or follow along on the Audio CD.
Respond Have students work in pairs or small groups to complete the Think It Over questions. Discuss the answer to the Analyze question. Encourage students to use the illustrations as evidence to support their opinions.
A Closer Look at… Draw students' attention to the photographs and captions on pages 206–207. Guide them to recognize that each photograph has a corresponding label and a caption. Have volunteers read the captions aloud as students follow along in their books. Then have students compare and contrast the bicycles.
Activity to Do Have students brainstorm a list of other machines that move people such as airplanes, motorcycles, cars, hot-air balloons, and the space shuttle. Have students select one of these machines to research.
Fluency Activity Do Fluency Activity 5 on page 164 of the *Teacher's Resource Book*.

Homework
Have students complete the Reader's Companion on *Workbook* page 122 and bring in pictures or photographs of the machine they chose.

Lesson 8

Common Core State Standards: RI.3.1, RI.3.3, RI.3.8, SL.3.6

Learning Strategies *Student Book* pages 208–209

- Use *Transparencies* 20 for Daily Language Practice, Week 20, Day 3.
- Use *Transparencies* 63 and page 149 of the *Teacher's Resource Book* for the T-Chart.

More about the Big Question Discuss how great ideas might have been helpful for students or their families and how many great ideas are the solutions to problems.
Problems and Solutions Students will practice identifying problems and solutions in a nonfiction reading. Ask: *What were the problems? How were they solved?*
Practice You may assign the practice activity as a class discussion, partner activity, or individual written assignment.
Use a T-Chart Let students know that this is not a problem and solution chart. List people or groups in one column. In the next column, students write how each person or group solved the problem of old bicycles being thrown away. Have students complete the graphic organizer and share their answers.
Apply In pairs, have students summarize the article. Encourage students to use the illustrations to help them. Listen for use of key words and vocabulary.
Extension Have students complete the extension activity and share it with the class. Have them explain why they would give their object away and why it might be beneficial to other people. Remind students to listen quietly while their classmates speak. Encourage them to ask questions after each presentation.

Homework
Have students do the Learning Strategies practice on *Workbook* page 123.

Lesson 9

Common Core State Standards: SL.3.1, SL.3.1.c, SL.3.6, L.3.1, .3.1.d

Grammar *Student Book* pages 210–211

- Use *Transparencies* 20 for Daily Language Practice, Week 20, Day 4.
- Have students complete the Unit 4, Reading 1 test in the *Assessments*.

***Need/want/like/love* + to + Verb** Read the introduction and refer to the chart to introduce the verbs + to + Verb. Have volunteers say a sentence using each one.
Practice Have students work individually. Then have them form small groups and check their answers. Encourage them to refer to the chart as they do so.
Apply Have students work in pairs to ask and answer the questions, using different verbs + to + Verb.

Homework
Have students complete the Grammar and Spelling exercises on *Workbook* pages 124–125.

Lesson 10

Common Core State Standards: W.3.2, W.3.2.a, W.3.4, W.3.5, W.3.10, SL.3.6

Writing *Student Book* pages 212–213

- Use *Transparencies* 20 for Daily Language Practice, Week 20, Day 5.
- Use *Transparencies* 63 and page 149 of the *Teacher's Resource Book* for the T-Chart.

Describe a Problem and Solution Brainstorm ideas about problems and solutions that students can write about.

Prewrite Give the students copies of the T-Chart, or have them copy one into their notebooks. Have them record the problem and solutions in the chart.

Draft Model how to turn the information in the chart into a draft by reading aloud the sample.

Writing Checklist Model how to use the Writing Checklist to help you improve the model paragraph you wrote. Encourage students to check for correct use of verbs. Have students trade papers and do a Peer Review, using the Checklist on page 402.

Homework

Have students prepare a final copy of their paragraph and do *Workbook* page 126.

Lesson 11

Common Core State Standards: RI.3.4, RI.3.7, SL.3.1, SL.3.1.c, SL.3.6, L.3.4, L.3.4.a, L.3.5.b

Reading 2 Key Words   *Student Book* pages 214–215

- Use *Transparencies* 21 for Daily Language Practice, Week 21, Day 1.
- Use *Transparencies* 47 for Key Words.

Prepare to Read Draw students' attention to the What You Will Learn section. Briefly discuss the topics that will be covered in this reading.

Key Words Read the key words aloud or play them on the Audio CD. Have students repeat each word as it is read aloud.

Words in Context Have students use the sentences and photographs as clues to help them understand the key words.

Visual Literacy Have students describe what they see in the photographs. Point out that photographs can help the reader understand words.

Practice Have students make flashcards to help them remember the meaning of the words and give them time to practice using their flashcards with a partner.

Apply Read aloud the text. Have students work in pairs to discuss the question and share their thoughts about smart pets.

Fluency Activity Do Fluency Activity 6 in the TE on page T214.

Homework

Have students complete the Key Words practice on *Workbook* page 127.

Lesson 12

Common Core State Standards: RI.3.4, RF.3.3, SL.3.1, SL.3.1.c, SL.3.6, L.3.4, L.3.4.a

Academic Words & Phonics   *Student Book* pages 216–217

- Use *Transparencies* 21 for Daily Language Practice, Week 21, Day 2.

Academic Words Discuss the definitions of the words and have students listen to the words in context on the Audio CD. Have students complete the Practice activity in their notebooks.

Apply Have students try to use the academic words when discussing the questions with a partner.

Phonics Play the Audio CD to show students about *R*-Controlled Vowels. Discuss the sound and ask students if they can think of other words that follow the same pattern. Have students complete the Practice section with a partner.

Homework

Have students complete the Academic Words and Phonics practice on *Workbook* pages 128–129.

Lesson 13

Common Core State Standards: RI.3.1, RI.3.2, RI.3.4, RI.3.7, RI.3.10

Reading 2 *Student Book* pages 218–223
• Use *Transparencies* 21 for Daily Language Practice, Week 21, Day 3.

More About the Big Question Read aloud the Big Question on page 218. Have students think about how people experiment, or try out ideas, to learn new things.
Audio Play the audio of the story, stopping to answer questions if students have them. Discuss the general meaning of the story and how it relates to the Big Question.
Reading Strategy Read aloud the bulleted items on page 218. Discuss how there is usually only one main idea in a selection and many details that support it. Encourage students to look for main ideas and details as they read the selection.
Genre Draw students' attention to the genre label. Point out that informational text is factual and that science books and social studies books are two examples of informational text.
Read Students can take turns reading the selection. Have them respond to the Before You Go On questions.
Onomatopoeia Direct attention to the words "Caw! Caw! Caw!" on page 218. Explain that some words in English sound the same as the actual noise they name. Introduce the term *onomatopoeia* and share these examples: *boom, quack, crash, buzz*. Have students call out other examples on onomatopoeia.
Fluency Activity Complete Fluency Activity 7 in TE on page T222.

Homework
Have students complete the Comprehension activities on *Workbook* page 130.

Lesson 14

Common Core State Standards: RI.3.1, RI.3.2, RI.3.4, RI.3.7, RI.3.10

Reading 2 *Student Book* pages 218–223
• Use *Transparencies* 21 for Daily Language Practice, Week 21, Day 4.
• Have students begin the Reader's Companion on page 131 of the *Workbook*.

Read Have students reread the story silently or listen to the Audio CD and follow along.
Reading Strategy Have students work in small groups to respond to the Reading Strategy questions on page 223.
Respond Have students work in pairs or small groups to complete the Think It Over questions. Discuss the answer to the Analyze question. Encourage students to use the illustrations as evidence to support their opinions.
Fluency Activity Complete Fluency Activity 8 in the TRB on page 164.

Homework
Have students complete the Reader's Companion on *Workbook* page 132.

Lesson 15

Common Core State Standards: RI.3.1, RI.3.2, SL.3.1, SL.3.1.c, SL.3.6

Learning Strategies *Student Book* pages 224–225
• Use *Transparencies* 21 for Daily Language Practice, Week 21, Day 5.
• Use *Transparencies* 55 and page 141 of the *Teacher's Resource Book* for the Main Idea/Supporting Details Chart.

More About the Big Question Discuss how the crows in the selection tried out their ideas.

Main Idea and Details Remind students that the main idea is the most important idea in the selection and that details tell about the main idea. Have students complete the Practice activity independently or in pairs.

Use a Main Idea/Supporting Details Chart Copy the chart on the board. Discuss the most important idea in the selection. Let students know they can refer to the selection to find details.

Apply In pairs, have students summarize the selection to a partner. Encourage students to use the illustrations to help them. Listen for use of key words and vocabulary in their summaries.

Extension Have students share their ideas with a partner. Invite each pair to share which animal they would like to learn about.

Homework

Have students complete the Learning Strategies practice on *Workbook* page 133.

Lesson 16

Common Core State Standards: SL.3.1, SL.3.1.c, SL.3.6, L.3.1, L.3.1.d, L.3.1.e

Grammar *Student Book* pages 226–227

• Use *Transparencies* 21 for Daily Language Practice, Week 21, Day 1.
• Have students complete the Unit 4, Reading 2 test in the *Assessments*.

Simple Past: Irregular Verbs Read the introduction and refer to the charts to introduce the irregular forms of simple past verbs. Have volunteers say a sentence using each one.

Practice Have students work individually. Then have them form small groups and check their answers. Encourage them to refer to the charts on page 226 as they do so.

Apply Have students work in pairs to ask and answer the questions, using the correct form of irregular simple past verbs.

Homework

Have students complete the Grammar and Spelling exercises on *Workbook* pages 134–135.

Lesson 17

Common Core State Standards: W.3.2, W.3.2.a, W.3.4, W.3.5, W.3.10

Writing *Student Book* pages 228–229

• Use *Transparencies* 21 for Daily Language Practice, Week 21, Day 2.
• Use *Transparencies* 59 and page 145 of the *Teacher's Resource Book* for the KWL Chart.

Respond to Text Read the writing prompt and discuss the text "Scientists and Crows."

Prewrite Ask students to think about the article. Give the students copies of the KWL Chart and have them fill in the columns.

Draft Read aloud the sample response to show students how to turn the ideas from the chart into their own response.

Writing Checklist Model how to use the Writing Checklist to help you improve the sample response. Have students trade papers and do a Peer Review, using the Checklist on page 402.

Homework

Have students prepare a final copy of their response and do the exercises on *Workbook* page 136.

Lesson 18

Common Core State Standards: RL.3.4, RL.3.7, SL.3.1, SL.3.1.c, SL.3.6, L.3.4, L.3.4.a, L.3.5.b

Reading 3 Key Words   *Student Book* pages 230–231

- Use *Transparencies* 21 for Daily Language Practice, Week 21, Day 3.
- Use *Transparencies* 48 for Key Words.

Prepare to Read Draw students' attention to the What You Will Learn section. Briefly discuss the topics that will be covered in this reading.
Key Words Read the key words aloud or play them on the Audio CD. Have students repeat each word as it is read aloud.
Words in Context Help students learn the skill of defining words by using context and illustrations to figure out the meaning of the highlighted words.
Practice Have students draw pictures of the key words and label each picture with a sentence.
Apply Read aloud the text. Have students work in pairs to discuss the questions and write their responses in their notebooks. Circulate and encourage students to use key words in their responses.
Fluency Activity Complete Fluency Activity 9 on TE page T230.

Homework
Have students complete the Key Words practice on *Workbook* page 137.

Lesson 19

Common Core State Standards: RI.3.4, RF.3.3, SL.3.1, SL.3.1.c, SL.3.6, L.3.3, L.3.4, L.3.4.a

Academic Words & Phonics   *Student Book* pages 232–233

- Use *Transparencies* 21 for Daily Language Practice, Week 21, Day 4.

Academic Words Discuss the definitions of the words and have students listen to the words in context on the Audio CD. Have students complete the Practice activity in their notebooks.
Apply Have students try to use the academic words when discussing the questions in the Apply section with a partner.
Phonics Read the text at the top of page 233 to introduce soft and hard *c*. Give several sample sentences where students listen for both sounds, and ask students to locate words in this or other selections that follow this pattern. Have students complete the Practice section with a partner.

Homework
Have students complete the Academic Words and Phonics practice on *Workbook* pages 138–139.

Lesson 20

Common Core State Standards: RI.3.1, RI.3.2, RI.3.4, RI.3.7, RI.3.10

Reading 3   *Student Book* pages 234–237

- Use *Transparencies* 21 for Daily Language Practice, Week 21, Day 5.

More About the Big Question To help students relate the Big Question to their own lives, have them consider what their own artwork says about who they are.
Audio Play the audio of the selection, stopping to answer questions if students have them. Discuss the general meaning and how it relates to the Big Question.

Reading Strategy Discuss with students how asking questions can help the reader better understand what a story is about. Read aloud the bulleted items on page 234. Encourage students to ask about each object's story.

Genre Draw students' attention to the genre. Remind students that a photo essay is a type of writing that uses photographs and captions to provide information.

Read Encourage students to refer to the illustrations as they read the story aloud. Use the Before You Go On as a reminder to ask questions.

Fluency Activity Do Fluency Activity 10 on TE page T236.

Homework
Have students complete the Think It Over Questions on page 237 in their notebooks.

Lesson 21

Common Core State Standards: RI.3.1, RI.3.2, RI.3.4, RI.3.7, RI.3.10

Reading 3 *Student Book* pages 234–237

- Use *Transparencies* 22 for Daily Language Practice, Week 22, Day 1.
- Have students complete the Reader's Companion on pages 140–141 of the *Workbook*.

Read Students may reread the story silently or listen to the Audio CD.

Reading Strategy Give students a concrete example of how to ask yourself questions as you read. Have groups respond to the Reading Strategy questions on page 237 and share their responses with the class. Be sure that each photo and caption is discussed.

Fluency Activity Complete Fluency Activity 11 in the TRB on page 164.

Homework
Have students complete the comprehension exercises on *Workbook* page 142.

Lesson 22

Common Core State Standards: RI.3.1, RI.3.2, SL.3.1.c, SL.3.6

Learning Strategies *Student Book* pages 238–239

- Use *Transparencies* 22 for Daily Language Practice, Week 22, Day 2.
- Use *Transparencies* 64 and page 149 of the *Teacher's Resource Book* for the T-Chart.

More About the Big Question Invite a discussion about how artwork or other creations show a person's ideas.

Ask Questions As a class, briefly review some question words that students may want to use to formulate their own questions. *What- What is it? Where- Where is it? Who- Who made it? How- How was it made? Why- Why is it important?*

Practice Before reading the passage, ask students to cover the questions below it. Have them read the questions after they have generated their own.

Use a T-Chart Ask students to think about the questions they have been asking about the selection. A T-Chart can help them organize the information they have gathered to better understand the selection.

Extension Have students draw the object for the Extension activity, label it, and prepare to present it to the class.

Homework
Have students do the Learning Strategies practice on *Workbook* page 143.

Lesson 23

Common Core State Standards: SL.3.1, SL.3.1.c, SL.3.6, L.3.1, L.3.1.a, L.3.1.b, L.3.2

Grammar   *Student Book* pages 240–241
- Use *Transparencies* 22 for Daily Language Practice, Week 22, Day 3.
- Have students complete the Unit 4, Reading 3 test in the *Assessments*.

Common and Proper Nouns Read the introduction and refer to the chart to introduce common and proper nouns. Have volunteers say a sentence using each one.
Practice Have students work individually. Then have them form small groups and check their answers. Encourage them to refer to the chart as they do so.
Apply Have students work in pairs to ask and answer the questions and identify whether the nouns in their answers are common or proper.

Homework
Have students complete the Grammar and Spelling exercises on *Workbook* pages 144–145.

Lesson 24

Common Core State Standards: W.3.2, W.3.2.a, W.3.4, W.3.5, W.3.10

Writing   *Student Book* pages 242–243
- Use *Transparencies* 22 for Daily Language Practice, Week 22, Day 4.
- Use *Transparencies* 58 and page 144 of the *Teacher's Resource Book* for the Sequence of Events Chart.

Explain a Process Read aloud the text at the top of page 242. Read the Writing Prompt aloud and discuss the types of things students can explain how to do.
Prewrite Give the students copies of the Sequence of Events Chart, or have them copy one into their notebooks. Encourage them to use common and proper nouns, as well as procedural words correctly.
Draft Read aloud the sample paragraph to show how to turn the ideas from the Sequence of Events Chart into written directions.
Writing Checklist Model how to use the Writing Checklist on page 243 to help you improve the sample. Encourage students to check for correct use of nouns and verbs. Have students trade papers and do a Peer Review, using the Checklist on page 402.

Homework
Have students prepare a final copy of their directions and do *Workbook* page 146.

Lesson 25

Common Core State Standards: RL.3.10, RI.3.9, RI.3.10, W.3.2, W SL.3.1, SL.3.1.c, SL.3.1.d, SL.3.6

Apply and Extend   *Student Book* pages 244–245
- Use *Transparencies* 22 for Daily Language Practice, Week 22, Day 5.

Link the Readings Discuss the genres of literature and informational text and the characteristics of each. Have students copy the chart on page 244 into their notebooks and complete it. Encourage students to identify the features of each genre to show their answers are correct.
Discussion Use the discussion questions to guide your class discussion, reviewing the readings and linking them together with the Big Question.

Projects Read aloud the choices for extension projects. Encourage students to be creative and to choose activities that suit their modalities. Have students begin working on their projects in class.

Homework
Have students finish their projects at home.

Lesson 26

Common Core State Standards: SL.3.1, SL.3.1.c, SL.3.2, SL.3.3, SL.3.4, SL.3.5, SL.3.6

Listening & Speaking Workshop, *Student Book* pages 246–247
Writing Workshop, *Student Book* page 248
- Use *Transparencies* 23 for Daily Language Practice, Week 23, Day 1.
- Use *Transparencies* 56 and page 142 of the *Teacher's Resource Book* for the Venn Diagram.

Prepare You may wish to use the Main Idea/Supporting Details Chart on *Teacher's Resource Book* page 141 to help students gather ideas about their hobby. Have students write a draft of their presentation on note cards.
Practice Give students time to practice their presentations. Encourage them to use visual aids and to memorize as much of it as they can.
Present After each presentation, allow the class to ask any questions they may have about what they heard.
Evaluate Have students answer the reflection questions in their notebooks or with a partner.
Writing Workshop Read aloud the writing prompt. Allow students to brainstorm things they can compare and contrast with a partner and then fill in their own graphic organizer with writing ideas.

Homework
Have students complete a draft of their compare and contrast essay.

Lesson 27

Common Core State Standards: W.3.2, W.3.2.a, W.3.2.b, W.3.2.c, W.3.2.d, W.3.4, W.3.5, W.3.10

Writing Workshop *Student Book* pages 248–250
- Use *Transparencies* 23 for Daily Language Practice, Week 23, Day 2.
- Have students complete the writing exercises on *Workbook* page 149.

Revise and Edit Read the sample draft aloud. Using the Writing Checklist, see if the class can make the writing more descriptive or find any errors. Encourage students to do this on their own, and then trade papers with a classmate to do a Peer Review. Circulate to give students feedback on their writing.
Project Allow students to share their unit projects with the class.

Homework
Have students create a final copy of their compare and contrast essay and complete *Workbook* page 150.

Lesson 28

Common Core State Standards: W.3.2, W.3.4, W.3.5, W.3.10, RF.3.4, RF.3.4.a, RF.3.4.b, RF.3.4.c

Writing Workshop, Fluency & Test Review *Student Book* page 251

- Use *Transparencies* 23 for Daily Language Practice, Week 23, Day 3.
- Use *Transparencies* 84 for Unit 4 Big Question to review the Big Questions for the unit.

Writing Workshop Allow students to share their published writing or post it in a central location where students can read each other's work.

Fluency Point out that you can practice fluency by reading a passage over and over until you read it smoothly. Have students listen to the sentences on the Audio CD and then practice reading them aloud smoothly.

Practice Working in pairs, have one student read the passage aloud while the other student listens and counts the number of words read in one minute. Circulate to help students identify words in the passage that slowed them down. Have students practice reading the passage several times to improve their reading rate.

Unit 4 Review Using the transparency, focus on the Big Questions for the unit. Review the unit's vocabulary, academic words, phonics, word study, and grammar topics to prepare for the Unit Test tomorrow. Have students complete *Workbook* pages 147–148.

Homework
Study for the Unit Test.

Lesson 29

Common Core State Standards: RI.3.1, RI.3.2, RI.3.3, RL.3.4, RI.3.7

Unit 4 Test *Student Book* pages 190–251

- Use *Transparencies* 23 for Daily Language Practice, Week 23, Day 4.

Test Have students complete the Unit 4 Test in the *Assessments*. Remind them that if they need to, they can use the *Student Book* to look up only the comprehension questions for the readings. Proctor students as they take the test, following the guide in *Assessments*.

Homework
Have students complete the Fluency activities on page 151 of the *Workbook*.

Lesson 30

Common Core State Standards: RL.3.1, RL.3.4, RI.3.1, RI.3.4

Test Preparation *Student Book* pages 252–253

- Use *Transparencies* 23 for Daily Language Practice, Week 23, Day 5.

Taking Tests Draw students' attention to the test format featured in this lesson.
Coaching Corner Guide students through the notes. Use the test sample on the facing page as a reference.
Practice Have students complete the test sample independently. Review it with the class and demonstrate how to apply the suggestions in the Tips box.

Homework
Have students complete the test preparation on *Workbook* pages 153–154.

Lesson 1

Common Core State Standards: RI.3.7, SL.3.1, SL.3.1.c, SL.3.6

Unit Opener   *Student Book* pages 254–255

• Use *Transparencies* 24 for Daily Language Practice, Week 24, Day 1.

Unit: Neighbors in Space Introduce the theme. Have students brainstorm a list of Earth's neighbors. Write the list on the board, and encourage discussion about related topics, such as astronauts. Build students' background on the unit theme by looking at the poster and playing the video.

Fluency Activity Post the Unit 5 Poster on the wall. Do Fluency Activity 1 at the bottom of TE page T254.

The Big Question Read the Big Question aloud. Encourage students to share their experiences about observing space.

Listening and Speaking Read the text in the box aloud. Explain that a TV newscast is a script that is read on TV and that they will do one later in the unit.

Writing Read the text aloud and tell students that they will do this later in the unit.

Quick Write Tell students to write one or two sentences, explaining why they think the moon changes its size and shape.

Homework

Ask students to take the Letter Home to their parents, explain it to them, and have their parents sign it.

Lesson 2

Common Core State Standards: RL.3.4, RI.3.4, RI.3.7, W.3.5, W.3.10, SL.3.1, SL.3.1.c, SL.3.6, L.3.4, L.3.4.a, L.3.5.b, L.3.4.d, L.3.6

What do you know about space?   *Student Book* pages 256–257

• Use *Transparencies* 24 for Daily Language Practice, Week 24, Day 2.

Words to Know Say each of the terms aloud. Encourage students to point to the correct illustration as they repeat each term with you. Direct students' attention to the Practice activity. Have students work in pairs and complete the sentence stem with the words provided. Ask students to complete the Write activity independently and share their answer with a partner.

Apply Guide students in getting information from the photos and labels. Read the sentence stems aloud and have students complete the sentences with the words provided.

What About You? Have students discuss the question with a partner. Encourage them to use the words they learned on these pages.

Homework

Have students answer the What About You question in their notebooks.

Lesson 3

Common Core State Standards: RI.3.7, SL.3.1, SL.3.1.c, SL.3.6

Kids' Stories from Around the World   *Student Book* pages 258–259

• Use *Transparencies* 24 for Daily Language Practice, Week 24, Day 3.

Kids' Stories from Around the World Read the children's stories. Students can also listen to the peer stories on the Audio CD. Use these stories as a model to help students talk and write about space.

Visual Literacy Have students follow the lines from the photographs on the page to the locations on the map. Say the names of each location and have students repeat the locations aloud. Encourage them to locate the same countries on other maps or globes.

What About You? Have students talk about their own experiences observing the moon and the stars.

Fluency Activity Do Fluency Activity 2 at the bottom of TE page T258.

Homework

Have students look at the sky and write their observations.

Lesson 4

Common Core State Standards: RI.3.4, RI.3.7, SL.3.1, SL.3.1.c, SL.3.6, L.3.4, L.3.4.a, L.3.5, L.3.5.b

Reading 1 Key Words *Student Book* pages 260–261

• Use *Transparencies* 24 for Daily Language Practice, Week 24, Day 4.
• Use *Transparencies* 49 for Key Words.

Prepare to Read Draw students' attention to the What You Will Learn section. Briefly discuss the topics that will be covered in this reading.

Key Words Read the key words aloud or play them on the Audio CD. Have students repeat each word as it is read aloud. Ask students what the words mean after they hear the sentences.

Words in Context Have students connect the sentences with the photographs.

Practice Have students make a new entry for their vocabulary notebooks and practice folding over the page to memorize the key words and definitions.

Apply Read the text aloud. Have students work in pairs to discuss their thoughts and feelings when they look at the night sky. Encourage them to use key words in their answers.

Fluency Activity Do Fluency Activity 3 at the bottom of TE page T260.

Homework

Have students complete the Key Words activities on *Workbook* page 155.

Lesson 5

Common Core State Standards: RI.3.4, RF.3.3, SL.3.1, SL.3.1.c, SL.3.6, L.3.4, L.3.4.a

Academic Words & Word Study *Student Book* pages 262–263

• Use *Transparencies* 24 for Daily Language Practice, Week 24, Day 5.

Academic Words Discuss the definitions of the words and have students listen to the words in context on the Audio CD. Have students complete the Practice activity in their notebooks.

Apply Have students try to use the academic words when discussing the questions in the Apply section with a partner.

Word Study Play the Audio CD to show students about synonyms and antonyms. Ask students if they can think of synonyms and antonyms for other words. Have students complete the Practice section with a partner.

Homework

Have students complete the Academic Words and Word Study practice on *Workbook* pages 156–157.

Lesson 6

Common Core State Standards: RI.3.1, RI.3.2, RI.3.4, RI.3.7, RI.3.10

Reading 1   *Student Book* pages 264–269

- Use *Transparencies* 25 for Daily Language Practice, Week 25, Day 1.

More about the Big Question To help students relate the Big Question to their own lives, review with students what they already know about space.
Audio Play the audio of the text, stopping to answer questions students may have. Discuss the general meaning of the selection and how it relates to the Big Question.
Reading Strategy Explain to students that reviewing what you already know about a topic can help you get ready to learn more about it. Model the strategy by sharing a few facts about space and writing some questions that you have. Have students generate a few questions about space and look for the answers to those questions as they read.
Read Have volunteers read the article aloud. Remind them to read the questions in the subheads, too. Other students can respond to the Before You Go On questions.
Fluency Activity Do Fluency Activity 5 at the bottom of TE page T14.

Homework
Have students complete the Comprehension activities on page 158 of the *Workbook*.

Lesson 7

Common Core State Standards: RI.3.1, RI.3.2, RI.3.4, RI.3.7, RI.3.10

Reading 1   *Student Book* pages 264–269

- Use *Transparencies* 25 for Daily Language Practice, Week 25, Day 2.
- Have students complete the Reader's Companion on page 159 of the *Workbook*.

Read Have students read the article aloud or follow along on the Audio CD.
Ask students to jot down any questions they have about the reading.
Numerical Data Call students' attention to the word *billions* on page 266. Write the number one billion on the board: 1,000,000,000. Use the script on page T266 of the *Teacher's Edition* to elicit discussion about the number.
Respond Have students work in pairs or small groups to complete the Think It Over questions. Discuss the answer to the Analyze question. Encourage students to use the illustrations as evidence to support their opinions.
Reading Strategy Have students work alone or in pairs to answer the questions on page 269. Ask students to share the things they wanted to know and any information they learned from the reading.

Homework
Have students complete the Reader's Companion on *Workbook* page 160.

Lesson 8

Common Core State Standards: RI.3.1, RI.3.2, SL.3.6

Learning Strategies   *Student Book* pages 270–271

- Use *Transparencies* 25 for Daily Language Practice, Week 25, Day 3.
- Use *Transparencies* 59 and page 145 of the *Teacher's Resource Book* for the KWL Chart.

More about the Big Question Discuss with students what information we can learn about space and how we can learn about it.

The 5W Questions Review with students the 5W Questions to help them set a purpose for reading. Have them complete the Practice activity with a partner. Encourage them to scan the story's headings to find the answers to the questions.

Use a KWL Chart Ask students to think about a day when they visited a museum. Ask them what they already knew before they entered. Ask if there was something more they wanted to know. Encourage students to conclude with what they learned that day in the museum. Have students complete the graphic organizer and share their answers.

Apply In pairs, have students summarize the selection. Encourage students to use the illustrations to help them. Listen for use of key words and vocabulary.

Extension Have students complete the Extension activity and share it with the class.

Homework

Have students do the Learning Strategies practice on *Workbook* page 161.

Lesson 9

Common Core State Standards: SL.3.1, SL.3.1.c, SL.3.6, L.3.1, L.3.1.i

Grammar   *Student Book* pages 272–273

- Use *Transparencies* 25 for Daily Language Practice, Week 25, Day 4.
- Have students complete the Unit 5, Reading 1 test in the *Assessments*.

Compound Sentences Read the introduction and refer to the chart to show students how to combine sentences. Have volunteers say a compound sentence using *and* or *but*.

Practice Have students work individually. Then have them form small groups and check their answers. Encourage them to refer to the chart as they do so.

Apply Have students work in pairs to ask and answer the questions, using compound sentences.

Homework

Have students complete the Grammar and Spelling exercises on *Workbook* pages 162–163.

Lesson 10

Common Core State Standards: W.3.1, W.3.1.a, W.3.4, W.3.5, W.3.10, SL.3.6

Writing   *Student Book* pages 274–275

- Use *Transparencies* 25 for Daily Language Practice, Week 25, Day 5.
- Use *Transparencies* 55 and page 141 of the *Teacher's Resource Book* for the Main Idea/Supporting Details Chart.

Write a Persuasive Paragraph Read the writing prompt aloud. As a class, discuss the reasons for and against learning about space.

Prewrite Give the students copies of the Main Idea/Supporting Details Chart, or have them copy one into their notebooks. Have them write their opinion in the main idea box and the supporting reasons in the boxes below.

Draft Model how to turn the information in the chart into a draft by reading the sample paragraph. Encourage students to use compound sentences in their writing.

Writing Checklist Model how to use the Writing Checklist to help you improve the model paragraph. Encourage students to use compound sentences. Have students trade papers and do a Peer Review using the Checklist on page 402.

Homework

Have students prepare a final copy of their paragraph and do *Workbook* page 164.

Lesson 11

Common Core State Standards: RL.3.4, RL.3.7, SL.3.1, SL.3.1.c, SL.3.6, L.3.4, L.3.4.a, L.3.5.b

Reading 2 Key Words   *Student Book* pages 276–277

- Use *Transparencies* 26 for Daily Language Practice, Week 26, Day 1.
- Use *Transparencies* 47 for Key Words.

Prepare to Read Draw students' attention to the What You Will Learn section. Briefly discuss the topics that will be covered in this reading.

Key Words Read the key words aloud or play them on the Audio CD. Have students repeat each word as it is read aloud.

Words in Context Have students use the sentences and photographs as clues to help them understand the key words.

Practice Have students illustrate the words and use them in sentences.

Apply Read the text aloud. Have students work in pairs to discuss what they like to observe in nature.

Fluency Activity Do the Fluency Activity in the TE on page T276.

Homework

Have students complete the Key Words practice on *Workbook* page 165.

Lesson 12

Common Core State Standards: RI.3.4, RF.3.3, SL.3.1, SL.3.1.c, SL.3.6, L.3.4, L.3.4.a

Academic Words & Word Study   *Student Book* pages 278–279

- Use *Transparencies* 26 for Daily Language Practice, Week 27, Day 2.

Academic Words Discuss the definitions of the words and have students listen to the words in context on the Audio CD. Have students complete the Practice activity in their notebooks.

Apply Have students try to use the academic words when discussing the questions in the Apply section with a partner.

Word Study Play the Audio CD to teach students about multiple-meaning words. Discuss the example and ask students if they can think of other words that have more than one meaning. Have students complete the Practice section with a partner.

Homework

Have students complete the Academic Words and Word Study practice on *Workbook* pages 166–167.

Lesson 13

Common Core State Standards: RL.3.1, RL.3.3, RL.3.4, RL.3.7, RL.3.9, RL.3.10, L.3.4, L.3.4.a, L.3.5.a, L.3.6

Reading 2   *Student Book* pages 280–283

- Use *Transparencies* 26 for Daily Language Practice, Week 26, Day 3.

More about the Big Question Read aloud the Big Question on page 280. Have students think about how people created stories to help them understand things about space.

Audio Play the audio of the story, stopping to answer questions if students have them. Discuss the general meaning of the story and how it relates to the Big Question.

Reading Strategy Read aloud the bulleted items on page 280. Explain that *compare* means to tell how things are alike; *contrast* tells how things are different. Tell students to follow the steps outlined as they read to compare and contrast different myths.

Genre Draw students' attention to the genre label. Explain that myths are fiction stories that give an explanation for natural events.
Read Students can take turns reading the selections aloud. At the end of each myth, have the students who listened tell the main points. Have them respond to the Before You Go On questions.
Fluency Activity Complete Fluency Activity 7 in TE on page T282.

Homework
Have students complete the Comprehension activities on *Workbook* page 168.

Lesson 14

Common Core State Standards: RL.3.1, RL.3.2, RL.3.3, RL.3.4, RL.3.7, RL.3.9, RL.3.10, L.3.4, L.3.4.a, L.3.5.a, L.3.6

Reading 2 *Student Book* pages 280–283
- Use *Transparencies* 26 for Daily Language Practice, Week 26, Day 4.
- Have students complete the Reader's Companion on page 169 of the *Workbook*.

Read Have students reread the myths silently or listen to the Audio CD and follow along.
Reading Strategy Give students a concrete example of how to compare and contrast. Have students work in small groups to respond to the Reading Strategy questions on page 283.
Respond Have students work in pairs or small groups to complete the Think It Over questions. Discuss the answer to the Analyze question. Encourage students to use the text and illustrations as evidence to support their opinions.
Fluency Activity Complete Fluency Activity 8 in the *Teacher's Resource Book* on page T164.

Homework
Have students complete the Reader's Companion on *Workbook* page 170.

Lesson 15

Common Core State Standards: RL.3.2, RL.3.9, W.3.3, SL.3.6

Learning Strategies *Student Book* pages 284–285
- Use *Transparencies* 26 for Daily Language Practice, Week 26, Day 5.
- Use *Transparencies* 56 and page 142 of the *Teacher's Resource Book* for the Venn Diagram.

More about the Big Question Discuss how myths may have helped people feel better about things they did not understand.
Compare and Contrast Remind students of the definitions of the words *compare* and *contrast.* Have students complete the Practice activity independently or in pairs.
Use a Venn Diagram Copy the chart on the board. Have students compare and contrast doing schoolwork with doing chores at home. Have them call out things that are similar and things that are different. Record student responses on the Venn Diagram. Have students reread the myths to complete the Venn Diagram.
Apply In pairs, have students retell the selection to a partner. Encourage students to use the illustrations to help them. Listen for use of key words and vocabulary in their retellings.
Extension Have students share their ideas about a new myth with a partner. Give students time to begin writing their myth.

Homework
Have students complete their myth and the practice activities on *Workbook* page 171.

Lesson 16

Common Core State Standards: SL.3.1, SL.3.1.c, SL.3.6, L.3.1, L.3.1.d, L.3.1.e

Grammar   *Student Book* pages 286–287
- Use *Transparencies* 27 for Daily Language Practice, Week 27, Day 1.
- Have students complete the Unit 5, Reading 2 test in the *Assessments*.

Future *be going to* Read the introduction and refer to the charts to introduce the correct forms to talk about the future. Have volunteers say a sentence using each one.
Practice Have students work individually. Then have them form small groups and check their answers. Encourage them to refer to the charts on page 286 as they do so.
Apply Have students work in pairs to ask and answer the questions, using the correct verb forms to talk about the future.

Homework
Have students complete the Grammar and Spelling exercises on *Workbook* pages 172–173.

Lesson 17

Common Core State Standards: W.3.1, W.3.4, W.3.5, W.3.10

Writing   *Student Book* pages 288–289
- Use *Transparencies* 27 for Daily Language Practice, Week 27, Day 2.
- Use *Transparencies* 55 and page 141 of the *Teacher's Resource Book* for the Main Idea/Support Details Chart.

Write a Prediction Read the writing prompt aloud and discuss what the students think and why. Record these predictions and reasons on the board.
Prewrite Give the students copies of the Main Idea/Supporting Details Chart, or have them copy one into their notebooks. Have them record their predictions and reasons in the chart.
Draft Read the sample paragraph aloud to show how to turn the ideas from the chart into their own response. Encourage students to use the future correctly.
Writing Checklist Model how to use the Writing Checklist to help you improve the sample response. Have students trade papers and do a Peer Review using the Checklist on page 402.

Homework
Have students prepare a final copy of their prediction and do the exercises on *Workbook* page 174.

Lesson 18

Common Core State Standards: RI.3.4, RI.3.7, SL.3.1, SL.3.1.c, SL.3.6, L.3.4, L.3.4.a, L.3.5.b

Reading 3 Key Words *Student Book* pages 290–291

- Use *Transparencies* 27 for Daily Language Practice, Week 27, Day 3.
- Use *Transparencies* 50 for Key Words.

Prepare to Read Draw students' attention to the What You Will Learn section. Briefly discuss the topics that will be covered in this reading.

Key Words Read the key words aloud or play them on the Audio CD. Have students repeat each word as it is read aloud.

Words in Context Help students learn the skill of defining words by using context and illustrations to define the highlighted words.

Practice Have students make flashcards for the key words and practice them with a partner.

Apply Read the text aloud. Have students work in pairs to discuss the questions and write their responses in their notebooks. Circulate and encourage students to use key words in their responses.

Fluency Activity Complete Fluency Activity 9 on TE page T290.

Homework

Have students complete the Key Words practice on *Workbook* page 175.

Lesson 19

Common Core State Standards: RI.3.4, RF.3.3, SL.3.1, SL.3.1.c, SL.3.6, L.3.3, L.3.4, L.3.4.a

Academic Words & Phonics *Student Book* pages 292–293

- Use *Transparencies* 27 for Daily Language Practice, Week 27, Day 4.

Academic Words Discuss the definitions of the words and have students listen to the words in context on the Audio CD. Have students complete the Practice activity in their notebooks.

Apply Have students try to use the academic words when discussing the questions in the Apply section with a partner.

Phonics Read the text at the top of page 293 to introduce *R*-Controlled vowels. Give several sample sentences where students listen for the sounds and then ask students to locate words in this or other selections that follow this pattern. Have students complete the Practice section with a partner.

Homework

Have students complete the Academic Words and Phonics practice on *Workbook* pages 176–177.

Lesson 20

Common Core State Standards: RI.3.1, RI.3.2, RI.3.4, RI.3.7, RI.3.10

Reading 3 *Student Book* pages 294–299

- Use *Transparencies* 27 for Daily Language Practice, Week 27, Day 5.

More about the Big Question Ask students how they think someone can become an astronaut. They will learn the answer by reading the biography.

Audio Play the audio of the selection, stopping to answer questions if students have them. Discuss the general meaning and how it relates to the Big Question.

Reading Strategy Explain to students that summarizing will help them understand what they have learned. They need to identify the main idea and important details in the selection in order to summarize.

Genre Draw students' attention to the genre. A biography is a true story about a person's life.

Read Have students take turns reading aloud. Invite them to look at the photos and illustrations and respond to the Before You Go On questions as they read.

Respond Have students work in pairs to answer the Think It Over questions on page 299.

Fluency Activity Do Fluency Activity 10 on TE page T298.

Homework

Have students complete the Comprehension activities on page 178 of the *Workbook*.

Lesson 21

Common Core State Standards: RI.3.1, RI.3.2, RI.3.4, RI.3.7, RI.3.10, SL.3.4, SL.3.6

Reading 3   *Student Book* pages 294–301

• Use *Transparencies* 28 for Daily Language Practice, Week 28, Day 1.

Read Students may reread the story silently or listen to the Audio CD.

Reading Strategy Help students summarize the selection. Have groups respond to the Reading Strategy questions on page 299 and share their responses with the class.

A Closer Look at… Draw students' attention to the captions beneath the photos. SAY *Read the captions and look at the pictures.* Ask the questions on page T301 of the *Teacher's Edition* to help students get information from the pictures.

Activity to Do Have students brainstorm other types of exploration in pairs or small groups. Have students look for pictures and write captions explaining the exploration they chose. Display the students' work.

Fluency Activity Complete Fluency Activity 11 in the TRB on page 164.

Homework

Have students complete the Reader's Companion on *Workbook* page 180.

Lesson 22

Common Core State Standards: RI.3.2, SL.3.1, SL.3.4, SL.3.6

Learning Strategies   *Student Book* pages 302–303

• Use *Transparencies* 28 for Daily Language Practice, Week 28, Day 2.
• Use *Transparencies* 55 and page 141 of the *Teacher's Resource Book* for the Main Idea/Supporting Details Chart.

More about the Big Question Invite a discussion about what students learned about becoming an astronaut.

Summarize Remind students that summarizing means identifying the main idea and important details of a reading. Tell students that they must read all of the details in the Practice activity before choosing the important ones. You may assign this as a class discussion, partner activity, or individual assignment.

Use a Main Idea/Supporting Details Chart Ask students to choose two details from number 1 to add to the Main Idea/Supporting Details Chart. They can reread the selection to help make their choices. Have them share their completed charts with a partner.

Apply Have students use their completed Main Idea/Supporting Details Chart to help them summarize the selection.

Extension Have students tell two or three details of what they did to make their dream come true. Ask them to tell a partner.

Homework

Have students do the Learning Strategies practice on *Workbook* page 181.

Lesson 23

Common Core State Standards: SL.3.1, SL.3.1.c, SL.3.6, L.3.1, L.3.1.i

Grammar *Student Book* pages 304–305

- Use *Transparencies* 28 for Daily Language Practice, Week 28, Day 3.
- Have students complete the Unit 5, Reading 3 test in the *Assessments*.

Complex Sentences: *because* and *so* Read the charts and text on page 304 to introduce using *because* and *so* to make complex sentences. Have students practice combining additional sample sentences orally.

Practice Have students work individually. Then have them form small groups and check their answers. Encourage them to refer to the chart as they do so.

Apply Have students work in pairs to ask and answer the questions, using complex sentences.

Homework

Have students complete the Grammar and Spelling exercises on *Workbook* pages 182–183.

Lesson 24

Common Core State Standards: W.3.1, W.3.1.a, W.3.4, W.3.5, W.3.10

Writing *Student Book* pages 306–307

- Use *Transparencies* 28 for Daily Language Practice, Week 28, Day 4.
- Use *Transparencies* 58 and page 144 of the *Teacher's Resource Book* for the Sequence of Events Chart.

Write a Persuasive Letter Read the writing prompt aloud. Brainstorm with the class some reasons for wanting information about Space Camp.

Prewrite Give the students copies of the Sequence of Events Chart, or have them copy one into their notebooks. Have them record their reasons for wanting information in the chart.

Draft Read the sample letter aloud to show how to turn the ideas from the chart into a persuasive business letter.

Writing Checklist Model how to use the Writing Checklist to help you improve the sample. Encourage students to check for correct use of the future and complex sentences. Have students trade papers and do a Peer Review using the Checklist on page 402.

Homework

Have students prepare a final copy of their letter and do *Workbook* page 184.

Lesson 25

Common Core State Standards: RL.3.9, RL.3.10, RI.3.9, RI.3.10, W.3.3, SL.3.1, SL.3.1.c, SL.3.1.d, SL.3.6

Apply and Extend   *Student Book* pages 308–309

• Use *Transparencies* 28 for Daily Language Practice, Week 28, Day 5.

Link the Readings Discuss the genres of literature and informational text and the characteristics of each. Have students copy the chart on page 308 into their notebooks and complete it. Encourage students to identify the features of each genre to show their answers are correct.

Discussion Use the discussion questions to help students review the readings and tie them together using the Big Question.

Projects Read aloud the choices for extension projects. Encourage students to be creative and to choose activities that suit their modalities. Have students begin working on their projects in class.

Homework

Have students finish their projects at home.

Lesson 26

Common Core State Standards: SL.3.1, SL.3.1.c, SL.3.2, SL.3.3, SL.3.4, SL.3.5, SL.3.6

Listening & Speaking Workshop,   *Student Book* pages 310–311
Writing Workshop

• Use *Transparencies* 29 for Daily Language Practice, Week 29, Day 1.
• Use *Transparencies* 61 and page 146 of the *Teacher's Resource Book* for the 5 W Chart.
• Use *Transparencies* 66 and page 151 of the *Teacher's Resource Book* for the Story Map.

Prepare Discuss the format of a TV newscast. First, have pairs of students complete the 5Ws Chart about their topic. Then, have them write out the script for it.

Practice Give students time to practice their newscasts. Encourage students to use visual aids in their presentations.

Present Prepare a desk at the front of the room where students can sit to present their newscasts.

Evaluate Have students answer the reflection questions in their notebooks or with a partner.

Writing Workshop Read the writing prompt aloud and discuss the books or movies that students could review. Allow students to brainstorm ideas for their reviews with a partner and then fill in their own Story Map with writing ideas.

Homework

Have students complete a draft of their review.

Lesson 27

Common Core State Standards: W.3.1, W.3.1.a, W.3.1.b, W.3.1.c, W.3.1.d, W.3.4, W.3.5, W.3.10

Writing Workshop   *Student Book* pages 312–314

• Use *Transparencies* 29 for Daily Language Practice, Week 29, Day 2.
• Have students complete the writing exercises on *Workbook* page 187.

Revise and Edit Read the sample draft aloud. Using the Writing Checklist, see if the class can make the writing more descriptive or find any errors. Encourage students to do this on their own, and then trade papers with a classmate to do a Peer Review. Circulate to give students feedback on their writing.

Project Allow students to share their unit projects with the class.

Homework
Have students create a final copy of their review and complete *Workbook* page 188.

Lesson 28

Common Core State Standards: W.3.1, W.3.4, W.3.5, W.3.10, RF.3.4, RF.3.4.a, RF.3.4.b, RF.3.4.c

Fluency & Test Review *Student Book* **page 315**
- Use *Transparencies* 29 for Daily Language Practice, Week 29, Day 3.
- Use *Transparencies* 85 for Unit 5 Big Question to review the Big Questions for the unit.

Writing Workshop Allow students to share their published writing or post it in a central location where students can read each other's work.
Fluency Point out that you can practice fluency by reading a passage over and over until you read it smoothly. Have students listen to the sentences on the Audio CD, and then practice reading them aloud smoothly.
Practice Working in pairs, have one student read the passage aloud while the other student listens and counts the number of words read in one minute. Circulate to help students identify words in the passage that slowed them down. Have students practice reading the passage several times to improve their reading rate.
Unit 5 Review Using the transparency, focus students' attention on the Big Questions for the unit. Take some time to review the unit's vocabulary, academic words, phonics, word study, and grammar topics to prepare for the Unit Test tomorrow. Have students complete *Workbook* pages 185–186.

Homework
Study for the Unit Test.

Lesson 29

Common Core State Standards: RL.3.1, RL.3.3, RL.3.4, RI.3.1, RI.3.2, RI.3.4

Unit 5 Test *Student Book* **pages 254–315**
- Use *Transparencies* 29 for Daily Language Practice, Week 29, Day 4.

Test Have students complete the Unit 5 Test in the *Assessments*. Remind students that if they need to, they can use the *Student Book* to go back and look up the comprehension questions to the readings, but they may not use the book for any other part of the test. Proctor students as they take the test, following the guide in *Assessments*.

Homework
Have students complete the Fluency activities on page 189 of the *Workbook*.

Lesson 30 **Common Core State Standards:** RI.3.1, RI.3.2, RI.3.4

Test Preparation *Student Book* **pages 316–317**
- Use *Transparencies* 29 for Daily Language Practice, Week 29, Day 5.

Homework
Have students complete the test preparation activities on *Workbook* pages 191–192.

Lesson 1

Common Core State Standards: RI.3.7, SL.3.1, SL.3.1.c, SL.3.6

Unit Opener   *Student Book* pages 318–319
• Use *Transparencies* 30 for Daily Language Practice, Week 30, Day 1.

Unit: Arts Festivals Introduce the theme. Tell students that they will read about arts festivals, or celebrations of different types of art. Build students' background on the unit theme by looking at the poster and playing the video.

Fluency Activity Post the Unit 6 Poster on the wall. Do Fluency Activity 1 at the bottom of TE page T318.

The Big Question Read the Big Question aloud. Encourage students to call out different types of art as you write it on the board.

Listening and Speaking Read the text in the box aloud. Ask students what they already know about making art. Invite students to talk about the types of art they like to make.

Writing Read the text aloud and tell students that they will do this later in the unit.

Quick Write Have students brainstorm the characters they might create in puppet form. Have students write about a puppet they would like to make.

Homework
Ask students to take the Letter Home to their parents, explain it to them, and have their parents sign it.

Lesson 2

Common Core State Standards: RL.3.4, RI.3.4, RI.3.7, W.3.5, W.3.10, SL.3.1, SL.3.1.c, SL.3.6, L.3.4, L.3.4.a, L.3.5.b, L.3.4.d, L.3.6

What do you know about arts festivals?   *Student Book* pages 320–321
• Use *Transparencies* 30 for Daily Language Practice, Week 30, Day 2.

Words to Know Say each of the terms aloud. Encourage students to point to the correct illustration as they repeat each term with you. Direct students' attention to the Practice activity. Have students work in pairs and complete the sentence stem with the words provided. Ask students to complete the Write activity independently and share their answer with a partner.

Apply Guide students in getting information from the photos and labels. Read the sentence stems aloud and have students complete the sentences with the words provided.

What About You? Have students discuss the question with a partner. Encourage them to use the words they learned on these pages.

Homework
Have students answer the What About You question in their notebooks.

Lesson 3

Common Core State Standards: RI.3.7, SL.3.1, SL.3.1.c, SL.3.6

Kids' Stories from Around the World   *Student Book* pages 322–323
• Use *Transparencies* 30 for Daily Language Practice, Week 30, Day 3.

Kids' Stories from Around the World Read the children's stories to learn about arts festivals around the world. Students can also listen to the peer stories on the Audio CD.

Visual Literacy Have students follow the lines from the photographs on the page to the locations on the map. Say the names of each location and have students repeat the locations aloud. Encourage them to locate the same countries on other maps or globes.

What about You? Refer to art projects you may have done in class. Have students pick one peer story and find similarities with their own experiences. Students can share their stories in small groups.
Fluency Activity Do Fluency Activity 2 at the bottom of TE page T322.

Homework
Have students write a story of their own using the peer stories as a model. Students can present their stories in small groups.

Lesson 4

Common Core State Standards: RI.3.4, RI.3.7, SL.3.1, SL.3.1.c, SL.3.6, L.3.4, L.3.4.a, L.3.5.b

Reading 1 Key Words   *Student Book* pages 324–325
• Use *Transparencies* 30 for Daily Language Practice, Week 30, Day 4.
• Use *Transparencies* 52 for Key Words.

Prepare to Read Draw students' attention to the What You Will Learn section. Briefly discuss the topics that will be covered in this reading.
Key Words Read the key words aloud or play them on the Audio CD. Have students repeat each word as it is read aloud. Ask students what the words mean after they hear the sentences.
Words in Context Have students connect the sentences with the photographs. Discuss how photographs can help with context clues.
Practice Have students make flashcards for the key words and allow them to practice memorizing the words and their definitions with a partner.
Apply Read the text aloud. Have students write about art they like to do.
Fluency Activity Do Fluency Activity 3 at the bottom of TE page T324.

Homework
Have students complete the Key Words activities on *Workbook* page 193.

Lesson 5

Common Core State Standards: RI.3.4, RF.3.3, SL.3.1, SL.3.1.c, SL.3.6, L.3.4, L.3.4.a

Academic Words & Phonics   *Student Book* pages 326–327
• Use *Transparencies* 30 for Daily Language Practice, Week 30, Day 5.

Academic Words Discuss the definitions of the words and have students listen to the words in context on the Audio CD. Have students complete the Practice activity in their notebooks.
Apply Have students try to use the academic words when discussing the questions in the Apply section with a partner.
Phonics Play the Audio CD to teach students about diphthongs. Ask students if they can think of other words that have this sound. Have students complete the Practice section with a partner.

Homework
Have students complete the Academic Words and Phonics practice on *Workbook* pages 194–195.

Lesson 6

Common Core State Standards: RI.3.1, RI.3.2, RI.3.4, RI.3.7, RI.3.10

Reading 1   *Student Book* pages 328–331

- Use *Transparencies* 31 for Daily Language Practice, Week 31, Day 1.

More about the Big Question The Big Question for this selection focuses on how and why people inform others about events through advertising.

Audio Play the audio of the text, stopping to answer questions students may have. Discuss the general meaning of the selection and how it relates to the Big Question.

Reading Strategy Discuss how identifying an author's purpose can help students better understand a selection. Make clear that *author's purpose* means the reason the author writes something.

Read Have volunteers read aloud the different sections of the selection. As a class, discuss how each of the sections relates to the arts festival.

Fluency Activity Do Fluency Activity 5 at the bottom of TE page T14.

Homework

Have students complete the Comprehension activities on page 196 of the *Workbook*.

Lesson 7

Common Core State Standards: RI.3.1, RI.3.2, RI.3.4, RI.3.7, RI.3.10

Reading 1   *Student Book* pages 328–331

- Use *Transparencies* 31 for Daily Language Practice, Week 31, Day 2.
- Have students complete the Reader's Companion on page 197 of the *Workbook*.

Read Have students read the article aloud or follow along on the Audio CD. Have students look for the author's purpose as they read.

Respond Have students work in pairs or small groups to complete the Think It Over questions. Discuss the answer to the Analyze question. Encourage students to use the illustrations as evidence to support their opinions.

Reading Strategy Have students work alone or in pairs to answer the questions on page 331. Ask students to share the things they wanted to know and any information they learned from the reading.

Homework

Have students complete the Reader's Companion on *Workbook* page 198.

Lesson 8

Common Core State Standards: RI.3.1, RI.3.2, SL.3.6

Learning Strategies   *Student Book* pages 332–333

- Use *Transparencies* 31 for Daily Language Practice, Week 31, Day 3.
- Use *Transparencies* 63 and page 149 of the *Teacher's Resource Book* for the T-Chart.

More about the Big Question Discuss with students why the poster for the arts festival was so important.

Author's Purpose Tell students that they can look for clues to the author's purpose in the main idea of a selection. Have a pair of students read each column of the chart. Have students suggest examples of writing for each purpose. Write a list on the board. Ask students to complete the Practice activity in pairs. Encourage them to review the selection before making a choice.

Use a T-Chart Have students complete the chart individually, and then discuss their responses in groups.

Apply In pairs, have students summarize the selection. Encourage students to use the illustrations to help them. Listen for use of key words and vocabulary.

Extension Have students complete the Extension activity and share it with a partner.

Homework

Have students do the Learning Strategies practice on *Workbook* page 199.

Lesson 9

Common Core State Standards: SL.3.1, SL.3.1.c, SL.3.6, L.3.2, L.3.2.b

Grammar   *Student Book* pages 334–335

- Use *Transparencies* 31 for Daily Language Practice, Week 31, Day 4.
- Have students complete the Unit 6, Reading 1 test in the *Assessments*.

Commas Read the introduction and refer to the chart to show students how to use commas. Have volunteers say a sentence that uses a comma and have the class listen for and identify the pause.

Practice Have students work individually. Then have them form small groups and check their answers. Encourage them to refer to the chart as they do so.

Apply Have students work in pairs to ask and answer the questions, using commas.

Homework

Have students complete the Grammar and Spelling exercises on *Workbook* pages 200–201.

Lesson 10

Common Core State Standards: W.3.2, W.3.2.a, W.3.4, W.3.5, W.3.7, W.3.8, W.3.10, SL.3.6

Writing   *Student Book* pages 336–337

- Use *Transparencies* 31 for Daily Language Practice, Week 31, Day 5.
- Use *Transparencies* 63 and page 149 of the *Teacher's Resource Book* for the T-Chart.

Plan a Research Report Discuss Task 1 with students. Brainstorm a list of topics that they can choose from. On one T-Chart, have students write their questions and answers. Model how to write more specific questions about the topic. Have students choose the question that is most interesting to them.

Make a Research Plan Using another T-Chart, have students list smaller questions about the topic and where they might find the answers to those questions.

Homework

Have students prepare a neat copy of their research plan and do *Workbook* page 202.

Lesson 11

Common Core State Standards: RI.3.4, RI.3.7, SL.3.1, SL.3.1.c, SL.3.6, L.3.4, L.3.4.a, L.3.5.b

Reading 2 Key Words   *Student Book* pages 338–339

- Use *Transparencies* 32 for Daily Language Practice, Week 32, Day 1.
- Use *Transparencies* 53 for Key Words.

Prepare to Read Draw students' attention to the What You Will Learn section. Briefly discuss the topics that will be covered in this reading.

Key Words Read the key words aloud or play them on the Audio CD. Have students repeat each word as it is read aloud.

Words in Context Have students use the sentences and photographs as clues to help them understand the key words.

Practice Have students illustrate the words and use them in sentences.

Apply Read the text aloud. Have students write about what they could make with the objects.

Fluency Activity Do Fluency Activity in TE on page T338.

Homework

Have students complete the Key Words practice on *Workbook* page 203.

Lesson 12

Common Core State Standards: RI.3.4, RF.3.3, SL.3.1, SL.3.1.c, SL.3.6, L.3.4, L.3.4.a

Academic Words & Phonics   *Student Book* pages 340–341

• Use *Transparencies* 32 for Daily Language Practice, Week 32, Day 2.

Academic Words Discuss the definitions of the words and have students listen to the words in context on the Audio CD. Have students complete the Practice activity in their notebooks.

Apply Have students try to use the academic words when discussing the questions in the Apply section with a partner.

Phonics Have a student volunteer read the words in the chart on page 341 or play the Audio CD to teach students the three sounds of the letter *y*. Point out the rules and ask students to share other words that follow the same patterns. Have students complete the Practice section with a partner.

Homework

Have students complete the Key Words and Phonics practice on *Workbook* pages 204–205.

Lesson 13

Common Core State Standards: RI.3.1, RI.3.2, RI.3.3, RI.3.4, RI.3.7, RI.3.10

Reading 2   *Student Book* pages 342–345

• Use *Transparencies* 32 for Daily Language Practice, Week 32, Day 3.

More about the Big Question The Big Question for this selection focuses on the importance of reading directions to help us learn how to do new things.

Audio Play the audio of the selection, stopping to answer questions if students have them. Discuss the general meaning of the text and how it relates to the Big Question.

Reading Strategy Read aloud the bulleted items on page 342. Discuss how steps in a process are connected and how paying attention to the order of the steps is important to the final product.

Genre Draw students' attention to the genre label. Point out that directions can appear in many places in school and at home.

Read Students can take turns reading the selection aloud. Have them respond to the Before You Go On question.

Fluency Activity Complete Fluency Activity 7 in TE on page T344.

Homework

Have students complete the Comprehension activities on *Workbook* page 206.

Lesson 14

Common Core State Standards: RI.3.1, RI.3.2, RI.3.3, RI.3.4, RI.3.7, RI.3.10

Reading 2 *Student Book* pages 342–347
• Use *Transparencies* 32 for Daily Language Practice, Week 32, Day 4.

Read Have students reread the directions silently or listen to the Audio CD and follow along.
Visual Literacy Refer students' attention to the photographs on pages 344 and 345. Ask how each photo helps them know what to do.
Reading Strategy Have students work in small groups to respond to the Reading Strategy questions on page 345.
Respond Have students work in pairs or small groups to complete the Think It Over questions. Discuss the answer to the Analyze question. Encourage students to use the text and illustrations as evidence to support their opinions.
A Closer Look at... Have students read the captions aloud while the class follows along, looking at the photographs. Discuss the purpose for reading this selection. Allow students time to complete the activity on page 347.
Fluency Activity Complete Fluency Activity 8 in the *Teacher's Resource Book* on page 164.

Homework
Have students complete the Reader's Companion on *Workbook* pages 207–208.

Lesson 15

Common Core State Standards: RI.3.2, RI.3.3, SL.3.6

Learning Strategies *Student Book* pages 348–349
• Use *Transparencies* 32 for Daily Language Practice, Week 32, Day 5.
• Use *Transparencies* 58 and page 144 of the *Teacher's Resource Book* for the Sequence of Events Chart.

More about the Big Question Discuss why reading directions are important when you are doing something new.
Reread for Details Discuss how looking back at a selection can help students clarify things they did not understand. Have students complete the Practice activity independently or in pairs.
Use a Sequence of Events Chart Copy the chart on the board. Encourage students to reread the selection to be sure they are placing the steps in the correct order.
Apply In pairs, have students retell the selection to a partner using their notes. Encourage students to use the illustrations to help them. Listen for use of key words and vocabulary in their retellings.

Homework
Have students complete the Learning Strategies practice on *Workbook* page 209.

Lesson 16

Common Core State Standards: SL.3.1, SL.3.1.c, SL.3.6, L.3.1, L.3.1.i

Grammar *Student Book* pages 350–351

- Use *Transparencies* 33 for Daily Language Practice, Week 33, Day 1.
- Have students complete the Unit 6, Reading 2 test in the *Assessments*.

The Imperative Read the introduction and refer to the charts to introduce the imperative. Have volunteers say a sentence using an imperative.
Practice Have students work individually. Then have them form small groups and check their answers. Encourage them to refer to the charts on page 350 as they do so.
Apply Have students work in pairs to ask and answer the questions, using the correct words.

Homework
Have students complete the Grammar and Spelling exercises on *Workbook* pages 210–211.

Lesson 17

Common Core State Standards: W.3.2, W.3.4, W.3.5, W.3.7, W.3.8, W.3.10

Writing *Student Book* pages 352–353

- Use *Transparencies* 33 for Daily Language Practice, Week 33, Day 2.

Include Paraphrases and Citations Read aloud the sample response, showing students how to paraphrase from a source.
Paraphrasing Have students write several paraphrased ideas from sources on index cards and be sure they have documented their sources correctly.

Homework
Have students do the exercises on *Workbook* page 212.

Lesson 18

Common Core State Standards: RI.3.4, RI.3.7, SL.3.1, SL.3.1.c, SL.3.6, L.3.4, L.3.4.a, L.3.5.b

Reading 3 Key Words *Student Book* pages 354–355

- Use *Transparencies* 33 for Daily Language Practice, Week 33, Day 3.
- Use *Transparencies* 86 for Key Words.

Prepare to Read Draw students' attention to the What You Will Learn section. Briefly discuss the topics that will be covered in this reading.
Key Words Read the key words aloud or play them on the Audio CD. Have students repeat each word as it is read aloud.
Words in Context Help students learn the skill of defining words by using context and illustrations to figure out the meaning of the highlighted words.
Practice Have students make flashcards for the key words and practice them with a partner.
Apply Read the text aloud. Have students work in pairs to discuss the questions and write their responses in their notebooks. Circulate and encourage students to use key words in their responses.
Fluency Activity Complete Fluency Activity 9 on TE page T354.

Homework
Have students complete the Key Words practice on *Workbook* page 213.

Lesson 19

Common Core State Standards: RI.3.4, RF.3.3, RF.3.3.c, SL.3.1, SL.3.1.c, SL.3.6, L.3.3, L.3.4, L.3.4.a

Academic Words & Word Study   *Student Book* pages 356–357

• Use *Transparencies* 33 for Daily Language Practice, Week 33, Day 4.

Academic Words Discuss the definitions of the words and have students listen to the words in context on the Audio CD. Have students complete the Practice activity in their notebooks.

Apply Have students try to use the academic words when discussing the questions in the Apply section with a partner.

Word Study Read the text at the top of page 357 to introduce multi-syllable words. Give several sample words where students listen for the number of syllables. Have students complete the Practice section with a partner.

Homework

Have students complete the Academic Words and Word Study practice on *Workbook* pages 214–215.

Lesson 20

Common Core State Standards: RI.3.1, RI.3.2, RI.3.4, RI.3.7, RI.3.10

Reading 3   *Student Book* pages 358–363

• Use *Transparencies* 33 for Daily Language Practice, Week 33, Day 5.

More about the Big Question Encourage students to think about the types of activities they would find at a music festival.

Audio Play the audio of the selection, stopping to answer questions if students have them. Discuss the general meaning and how it relates to the Big Question.

Reading Strategy Read aloud the text on page 358 and model the strategy. Discuss the conclusions that can be made and the reasons for them.

Read Have students take turns reading aloud. Invite them to look at the photos and illustrations and respond to the Before You Go On questions as they read.

Fluency Activity Do Fluency Activity 10 on TE page T362.

Homework

Have students complete the Comprehension activities on page 216 of the *Workbook*.

Lesson 21

Common Core State Standards: RI.3.1, RI.3.2, RI.3.4, RI.3.7, RI.3.10

Reading 3   *Student Book* pages 358–363

• Use *Transparencies* 34 for Daily Language Practice, Week 34, Day 1.
• Have students begin the Reader's Companion on page 217 of the *Workbook*.

Read Students may reread the story silently or listen to the Audio CD.

Reading Strategy Review the answers to the 5W questions with students. Discuss the conclusions that can be drawn from those details. Have students respond to the Reading Strategy questions in their notebooks.

Respond Have students work in pairs to answer the Think It Over questions on page 363.

Fluency Activity Complete Fluency Activity 11 in the TRB on page 164.

Homework

Have students complete the Reader's Companion on *Workbook* page 218.

Lesson 22

Common Core State Standards: RI.3.1, RI.3.2, RI.3.3, SL.3.6

Reading 3   *Student Book* **pages 364–365**

- Use *Transparencies* 34 for Daily Language Practice, Week 34, Day 2.
- Use *Transparencies* 61 and page 146 of the *Teacher's Resource Book* for the 5W Chart.

More about the Big Question Have students work in pairs to answer the Big Question.
Draw a Conclusion Have students work in pairs to answer the questions in the Practice section. Discuss the conclusions that students came to and the reasons for them.
Use a Main Idea/Supporting Details Chart Have students complete the chart independently and share their conclusions with the class.
Apply Ask students to use the answers to the 5W questions to help them summarize the selection to a partner.
Extension Have students prepare a dance to their favorite music and perform it for the class. Alternatively, students can write about an experience they had at a concert or music festival.

Homework
Have students do the Learning Strategies practice on *Workbook* page 219.

Lesson 23

Common Core State Standards: SL.3.1, SL.3.1.c, SL.3.6, L.3.2, L.3.2.c

Grammar   *Student Book* **pages 366–367**

- Use *Transparencies* 34 for Daily Language Practice, Week 34, Day 3.
- Have students complete the Unit 6, Reading 3 test in the *Assessments*.

Quotations Read the text and charts on page 366 to show students how to use quotations correctly. Have students speak to you. Write down what they say and have volunteers come up and write in the quotation marks.
Practice Have students work individually. Then have them form small groups and check their answers. Encourage them to refer to the chart as they do so.
Apply Have students work in pairs to ask and answer the questions, using quotations.

Homework
Have students complete the Grammar and Spelling exercises on *Workbook* pages 220–221.

Lesson 24

Common Core State Standards: W.3.2, W.3.4, W.3.5, W.3.7, W.3.8, W.3.10, L.3.2, L.3.2.c

Writing   *Student Book* **pages 368–369**

- Use *Transparencies* 34 for Daily Language Practice, Week 34, Day 4.

Include Quotations and Citations Read aloud the text and sample on page 368 to show students how to include quotations in their research reports. Have students continue researching and locate quotes that they wish to include in their reports. Have them begin the first draft of the report, including paraphrased information and quotations.

Homework
Have students continue researching and drafting their reports and do *Workbook* page 222.

Lesson 25

Common Core State Standards: RL.3.9, RL.3.10, RI.3.9, RI.3.10, W.3.2, W.3.3, SL.3.1, SL.3.1.c, SL.3.1.d, SL.3.4, SL.3.6

Apply and Extend   *Student Book* pages 370–371

• Use *Transparencies* 34 for Daily Language Practice, Week 34, Day 5.

Link the Readings Discuss the genres of literature and informational text and the characteristics of each. Have students copy the chart on page 370 into their notebooks and complete it. Encourage students to identify the features of each genre to show their answers are correct.

Discussion Use the discussion questions to help students review the readings and tie them together with the Big Question.

Projects Read aloud the choices for extension projects. Encourage students to be creative and to choose activities that suit their modalities. Have students begin working on their projects in class.

Homework

Have students finish their projects at home.

Lesson 26

Common Core State Standards: SL.3.1, SL.3.1.c, SL.3.2, SL.3.3, SL.3.4, SL.3.5, SL.3.6

Listening & Speaking Workshop,   *Student Book* pages 372–373
Writing Workshop, *Student Book* page 374

• Use *Transparencies* 35 for Daily Language Practice, Week 35, Day 1.

Prepare Read aloud the text at the top of page 372. Discuss the types of things that students can present to the class. You may wish to have them plan their presentations on a Sequence of Events Chart (*TRB,* page 144). Encourage students to use props or visual aids to help them show the class how to do something.

Practice Give students time to practice their presentations.

Present Encourage students to speak clearly and use their visual aids to show the class how to do something.

Evaluate Have students answer the reflection questions in their notebooks or with a partner.

Writing Workshop Read aloud the text on page 374. Have students assemble their research and begin working on an outline. You may wish to have students use an extended version of a Main Idea/Supporting Details Chart (*TRB,* page 141) to record their ideas.

Homework

Have students complete a draft of their research report.

Lesson 27

Common Core State Standards: W.3.2, W.3.4, W.3.5, W.3.7, W.3.8, W.3.10

Writing Workshop   *Student Book* pages 374–375

• Use *Transparencies* 35 for Daily Language Practice, Week 35, Day 2.
• Have students complete the writing exercises on *Workbook* page 225.

Revise and Edit Read the sample draft aloud. Using the Writing Checklist, see if the class can make the writing more descriptive or find any errors. Encourage students

to do this on their own, and then trade papers with a classmate to do a Peer Review. Circulate to give students feedback on their writing.
Project Allow students to share their unit projects with the class.

Homework
Have students create a final copy of their research report and complete *Workbook* page 226.

Lesson 28

Common Core State Standards: W.3.2, W.3.4, W.3.5, W.3.10, RF.3.4, RF.3.4.a, RF.3.4.b, RF.3.4.c

Fluency & Test Review *Student Book* page 379
- Use *Transparencies* 35 for Daily Language Practice, Week 35, Day 3.
- Use *Transparencies* 86 for Unit 6 Big Question to review the Big Questions for the unit.

Writing Workshop Allow students to share their published writing or post it in a central location where students can read each other's work.
Fluency Point out that you can practice fluency by reading a passage over and over until you read it smoothly. Have students listen to the sentences on the Audio CD and then practice reading them aloud smoothly.
Practice Working in pairs, have one student read the passage aloud while the other student listens and counts the number of words read in one minute. Circulate to help students identify words in the passage that slowed them down. Have students practice reading the passage several times to improve their reading rate.
Unit 6 Review Using the transparency, focus students' attention on the Big Questions for the unit. Take some time to review the unit's vocabulary, academic words, phonics, word study, and grammar topics to prepare for the Unit Test tomorrow. Have students complete *Workbook* pages 223–224.

Homework
Study for the Unit Test.

Lesson 29

Common Core State Standards: RI.3.1, RI.3.2, RI.3.3, RI.3.7

Unit 6 Test *Student Book* pages 256–381
- Use *Transparencies* 35 for Daily Language Practice, Week 35, Day 4.

Test Have students complete the Unit 6 Test in the *Assessments*. Remind students that if they need to, they can use the *Student Book* to go back and look up the comprehension questions to the readings, but they may not use the book for any other part of the test. Proctor students as they take the test, following the guide in *Assessments*.

Homework
Have students complete the Fluency activities on page 227 of the *Workbook*.

Lesson 30

Test Preparation   *Student Book* pages 380–381

• Use *Transparencies* 35 for Daily Language Practice, Week 35, Day 5.

Homework

Have students complete the test preparation activities on *Workbook* pages 229–230.

WORKBOOK
ANSWER KEYS

Unit 1

Page 3 • KEY WORDS
A.

1. luck
2. flower
3. mail
4. street
5. neat

B.

6. mail
7. luck
8. street
9. flowerhh
10. neat

Page 4 • ACADEMIC WORDS
A.

1. k m z purchase g n w
2. d b c o n s item a p l y r

B.

3. purchase
4. item
5. purchase
6. item

C.

7. Answers will vary.
8. Answers will vary.

Page 5 • PHONICS
A.

1. van
2. bad, bed, bid, bud
3. lap, lip
4. hat, hit, hot, hut
5. cat, cot, cut
6. bus

B.

7. can, run
8. can, fun
9. let
10. can, sit

Page 6 • COMPREHENSION

1. dog
2. mail or letters
3. Gus
4. **Possible response:** He is friendly. He thinks of others. He can catch a disk.
5. **Possible response:** He's a nice guy. He loves her.

Page 7 • READER'S COMPANION
Possible responses
Use What You Know
my friend Emil, Mr. Boca at the corner store, my neighbor Jessie
Reading Strategy
Hector is friendly. Underline: To lots of people on his way, He says "¡Hola! How's your day?"
Genre
Circle two of the following pairs: way, day; park, bark; fly, try.

Page 8
Possible responses
Use the Strategy
I think Hector likes living in his city. He talks to people and he plays in the park.
Retell It!
I skipped along the street. I said "¡Hola!" to my friends. I caught a disk a man threw in the park.
Reader's Response
I would like to play in the park with the dog.

Page 9 • LEARNING STRATEGIES

1. She takes the dog to the park. She brings the dog home. She gives it food and water.
2. b

Page 10 • GRAMMAR
A.

1. are
2. is
3. am
4. are
5. am

B.

1. He's
2. I'm
3. We're
4. You're

Page 11 • SPELLING
A.

1. man, men
2. cap, cop, cup
3. dig, dog, dug

B.
Possible responses (choose two)

4. dog, fog, jog, hog, log
5. rub, rug, run, rut
Writing Activity
Possible response: I have a pet cat. I have fun with my cat. My cat can run and jump.

Page 12 • WRITING

1. B
2. C
3. D

Page 13 • KEY WORDS
A.

1. dessert
2. mix
3. friend
4. fold

B.

F	R	I	E	N	D	T
X	K	O	I	N	E	D
C	Q	A	W	X	S	M
R	F	N	I	A	S	E
W	O	M	T	K	E	U
C	L	E	L	Z	R	R
D	D	Y	Z	E	T	F

Page 14 • ACADEMIC WORDS
A.

1. k m z p u r create k l p t
2. d b c o n s i task a p l y r

B.

3. create
4. create
5. task
6. task

C.

7. Answers will vary.
8. Answers will vary.

Page 15 • PHONICS

1. same
2. mice
3. like, slide
4. hope
5. bake
6. ride
7. snake
8. five
9. close

Page 16 • COMPREHENSION

1. Japan
2. bird
3. dessert
4. She got the things together. She cooked the dessert.
5. Possible answer: They taught each other a fun thing.

Page 17 • READER'S COMPANION
Use What You Know
Possible response: 1. Alina 2. Dina 3. Juan
Reading Strategy
Hana says she can make paper animals.
Comprehension Check
Hana just came to this school.
Carlos just came here.

Page 18
Possible responses
Use the Strategy
1. Miss Jones tells Carlos to sit by Hana.
2. Hana says she can make paper animals.
Retell It!
I made a friend. His name is Carlos. I showed him how to make a paper animal.
Reader's Response
I know jump rope games. I can teach my friends how to jump rope. I can teach the songs.

Page 19 • LEARNING STRATEGIES

5
3
2
1
4

Page 20 • GRAMMAR
A.

1. goes
2. sits
3. play
4. reads
5. eat

B.

6. cooks
7. make
8. gets
9. walk

Page 21 • SPELLING
Possible responses

1. Juan
2. Mr. Anders
3. Jose Marti Elementary School
4. September
5. Fourth of July
6. Oregon
7. United States
8. Saturday
Writing Activity
Possible response: I go to Rosa Parks Elementary school. I am in Ms. Garza's class. My best friend is Ella.

Page 22 • WRITING

1. A
2. D
3. A

Page 23 • KEY WORDS

A.

1. company
2. gathers
3. celebrate
4. crowd
5. weekend

B.

6. weekend
7. crowd
8. gathers
9. celebrate
10. company

Page 24 • ACADEMIC WORDS

1. c o n t r i b u t e a t e k l p t
2. d b c o n s i m i l a r i n g l t

B.

3. similar
4. contribute
5. contribute
6. similar

C.

7. Answers will vary. 8. Answers will vary.

Page 25 • WORD STUDY

1. B
2. A
3. B
4. B

Page 26 • COMPREHENSION

1. The family gets together.
2. They celebrate Grandmother's birthday.
3. Candles are on top of the cake.
4. Possible answers: They put up streamers. Mom bakes a cake. Everyone brings presents. Dad cooks. Mom makes salad.
5. They are fun because the whole family gathers together.

Page 27 • READER'S COMPANION

Possible responses

Use What You Know

1. mother 2. sister 3. grandmother

Reading Strategy

1. tamales 2. soup 3. flan

Comprehension Check

salad lemonade

Page 28

Possible responses

Use the Strategy

We play a card game, Go Fish. You ask a player for a certain card. If she doesn't have it, she says "Go fish!"

Retell It!

I went to a party. It was in my neighbor's yard. We ate good food and drank lemonade. We played games.

Reader's Response

I think the celebration took place in the summer. It was held in the yard. Everyone was drinking lemonade.

Page 29 • LEARNING STRATEGIES

Possible responses

1. On Saturday we play soccer. On Sunday we see my cousins.
2. I wash the dishes. I feed the dog, too.

Page 30 • GRAMMAR

1. candles
2. dishes
3. flowers
4. families
5. buses

6. babies
7. legs

Page 31 • SPELLING

1. cities
2. parties
3. stories
4. families
5. buddies
6. puppies
7. babies

Writing Activity

Possible response: In my family, we all have hobbies. My sister writes stories. My grandmother knits socks for babies. I act out plays with my buddies.

Page 32 • WRITING

1. A
2. C
3. D

Pages 33–34 • REVIEW

1. **Possible response:** He says "hola" to everyone.
2. D
3. B
4. B
5. **Possible response:** The mother bakes a cake. The girl and her cousins put up streamers. They give the grandmother gifts. They sing to her.
6. C
7. **Possible response:** We sing the birthday song when we have family parties, too.

Pages 35–36 • WRITING WORKSHOP

1. D
2. A
3. B
4. C
5. A

Page 39 • TEST PREPARATION

1. clock
2. a student in the class
3. goes on

Page 40

1. neighborhood
2. making new friends

Unit 2

Page 41 • KEY WORDS

A.

1. well
2. roars
3. reflection
4. dinner

B.

5. twe dinner tion
6. pdflpital well
7. pwdwn roar solpe
8. da reflection hx

Page 42 • ACADEMIC WORDS

A.

1. k f o c u s o i n t e r a c t l i t
2. o u i d e n t i f y i g d o m

B.

3. FALSE
4. TRUE

5. TRUE
6. TRUE

C.

7. Answers will vary.
8. Answers will vary.

Page 43 • PHONICS

A.

1. boat; circle *oa*
2. fruit; circle *ui*
3. clue; circle *ue*
4. toe; circle *oe*

B.

5. *oa*
6. *oe*
7. *ue*
8. *ui*

Page 44 • COMPREHENSION

1. rabbit
2. his reflection
3. an echo
4. Lion wants to get rid of the lion in the well.
5. Rabbit has tricked Lion.

Page 45 • READER'S COMPANION

Use What You Know

Possible response: 1. fruit 2. cheese

Reading Strategy

Look at the lion in the well. He says he is king!

Comprehension Check

dinner snack

Page 46

Possible responses

Use the Strategy

yells for help; tries to trick Lion

Retell It!

Ow! Lion finally caught me and wanted to eat me. But I tricked him because I am smart!

Reader's Response

I would yell for help and try to get away.

Page 47 • LEARNING STRATEGIES

A lion catches a mouse. The lion laughed so hard he let the mouse go. The next day, a hunter caught the lion. The hunter tied the lion to a tree. The mouse chewed through the rope and set the lion free.

Page 48 • GRAMMAR

A.

1. his
2. Her
3. It's
4. his
5. his

B.

6. her
7. their
8. his

Page 49 • SPELLING

1. off
2. than
3. then
4. of

Writing Activity

Possible response: I will remember how each word is used in a sentence.

Page 50 • WRITING

1. C
2. B
3. D

Page 51 • KEY WORDS

A.

1. clouds
2. stronger
3. webs
4. spiders
5. brighter

B.

6. brighter
7. spiders
8. clouds
9. webs
10. stronger

Page 52 • ACADEMIC WORDS

A.

1. k f o c u s o i n t affect
2. a f o u attitude o m

B.

3. TRUE
4. FALSE
5. TRUE
6. TRUE

C.

7. Answers will vary. 8. Answers will vary.

Page 53 • WORD STUDY

A.

1. fearless
2. dishonest
3. dislike
4. careless

B.

5. C
6. D
7. B
8. E
9. F
10. A

Page 54 • COMPREHENSION

1. North Wind and Sun
2. Sun
3. takes off her hat
4. He cools her off.
5. **Possible response:** Every person has gifts to share.

Page 55 • READER'S COMPANION

Possible responses

Use What You Know

The wind can be cold. The wind can bring rain.

Reading Strategy

The North wind took another breath and then she blew very hard.

Comprehension Check

She blew leaves from the trees.

She pushed flying birds from the sky.

Page 56

Possible responses

Use the Strategy

I picture the wind puffing out her cheeks. She is angry. She tries hard to blow off the woman's hat.

Retell It!

Whoa! That is a strong wind! It blew me out of my web. My web is blowing away, too.

Reader's Response

I would hide behind a big tree.

Page 57 • LEARNING STRATEGIES

Possible responses

1. I picture a young girl who runs very fast. The wind blows through her hair as she runs.

2. Annie is also a fast runner. She is wearing shorts.

Page 58 • GRAMMAR

1. walked
2. played
3. cooked
4. jumped
5. shouted
6. cried
7. skipped
8. studied
9. laughed
10. petted

Page 59 • SPELLING

1. crew
2. blue
3. new
4. clue
5. few

Writing Activity

The space crew took off into the blue sky in a new shuttle.

Page 60 • WRITING

1. B
2. A
3. C

Page 61 • KEY WORDS

A.

1. soil
2. garden
3. seeds
4. plants

B.

a	m	l	p	c	x	d	w	m	r	f	s
t	r	s	g	s	h	r	u	r	b	g	e
y	g	h	m	d	r	s	p	f	s	r	e
n	e	i	g	h	b	o	r	h	o	o	d
d	t	f	a	r	j	i	z	d	n	d	s
e	x	b	r	t	p	l	a	n	t	s	m
j	g	g	d	x	t	t	i	x	h	t	s
l	h	f	e	s	h	y	j	n	g	h	x
p	l	e	n	v	d	k	n	g	r	m	r
t	s	t	n	t	v	b	g	o	p	v	t
d	b	d	s	p	t	s	h	r	d	p	s
s	n	g	v	g	z	b	n	v	t	d	g

Page 62 • ACADEMIC WORDS

A.

1. k m o p interact f r p l
2. d outcome t l d m p

B.

3. TRUE
4. TRUE
5. FALSE
6. FALSE

C.

7. Answers will vary.
8. Answers will vary.

Page 63 • PHONICS

A.

Long *a* Pairs: stay, circle ay; rain, circle ai

Long *e* Pairs: clean, circle ea; seed, circle ee; week, circle ee

Long *i* Pairs: cried, circle ie; skies, circle ie; pie, circle ie

B.

1. need
2. lie
3. clay
4. eat
5. train
6. neat

Page 64 • COMPREHENSION

1. a garden grown by a group of people
2. make a list of what needs to be done
3. to remove the weeds
4. Gardens are neat and plants are pretty to look at.
5. people work together

Page 65 • READER'S COMPANION

Possible responses

1. fresh vegetables make people healthier
2. fresh air makes people healthier
3. exercise makes people healthier

Reading Strategy

Gardens make neighborhoods look more beautiful. Having a community garden in their neighborhood gives them the chance to see something beautiful everyday.

Comprehension Check

community, neighborhood

Page 66

Possible answers

Use the Strategy

Community gardens can help improve people's lives.

By eating fresh vegetables, gardeners may become healthier.

They can enjoy lots of fresh air and exercise, too.

Sometimes city people don't have a chance to enjoy nature.

Retell It!

Come work in a community garden. It will make you healthy. You will get fresh air. You will exercise. And you will get good vegetables to eat.

Reader's Response

Answers will vary.

Page 67 • LEARNING STRATEGIES

1. Mom and Dad had a good idea. Everyone liked the idea of a community garden. That was the best job.
2. Answers will vary.

Page 68 • GRAMMAR

1. were
2. is
3. am
4. were
5. was
6. are
7. were

Page 69 • SPELLING

Possible responses

A.

1. may
2. weigh
3. say
4. paid
5. wait
6. eight

B.

neighborhood, eight, hay, neigh, trail

Writing Activity

I like to walk on the trail in my neighborhood in May to pick flowers.

Page 70 • WRITING

1. B
2. A
3. C

Pages 71–72 • REVIEW
1. B
2. A reflection is an image that shows on a shiny or clear surface.
3. The Sun is calm and friendly. He smiles even when he is making the weather hot.
4. D
5. The Sun and Rabbit do not try to be strong. They are smart.
6. **Possible responses:** to make the neighborhood more beautiful; to make them healthier; to get some exercise
7. A

Page 73–74 • WRITING WORKSHOP
1. A   4. A
2. C   5. D
3. B

Page 77 • TEST PREPARATION
1. spines
2. The prickly pear cactus is a tough plant!

Page 78
1. dirt
2. to grow plants and work together

Unit 3

Page 79 • KEY WORDS
A.
1. plains
2. caves
3. camels
4. amazing
5. habit
B.
6. camels
7. amazing
8. habits
9. plains
10. caves

Page 80 • ACADEMIC WORDS
A.
1. k m (appreciates) l
2. d g a r d p k (illustrate)
B.
3. FALSE
4. TRUE
5. TRUE
6. FALSE
C.
7. Answers will vary.
8. Answers will vary.

Page 81 • PHONICS
Possible responses
1. broom, groom, bloom, gloom
2. smile
3. tree, flee, free, glee
4. drape, grape

5. clay, gray, pray, tray, stay, sway, play
6. press, dress, bless
7. sleep, creep, bleep, steep, sweep
8. trip, drip, grip, skip, snip, clip, flip, slip, blip
9. blue, glue, clue, true, flue
10. swim, trim, skim, slim, brim, grim

Page 82 • COMPREHENSION
1. cats, dogs, and rabbits
2. rested
3. frog
4. Animals will choose homes best suited for their different habits.
5. Ali went looking for food.

Page 83 • READER'S COMPANION
1. cats
2. dogs
3. rabbits
Reading Strategy
(Animals live all over the world in many kinds of homes.)
Comprehension Check
(caves) (trees)

Page 84
Possible answers
Use the Strategy
Tame animals can be kept at home. They are not wild. They need us to care for them.
Retell It!
We are all different. We live in different kinds of homes. Some of us live with people. Some of us live in trees.
Reader's Response
Answers will vary.

Page 85 • LEARNING STRATEGIES
Birds do a good job caring for their young.

Page 86 • GRAMMAR
1. under, on   5. above
2. on   6. at
3. in   7. between
4. near   8. on

Page 87 • SPELLING
1. making
2. sharing
3. living
4. hiking
5. writing
Writing Activity
Possible response: The mouse is hiding from the cat. The dog is chasing the bird.

Page 88 • WRITING
1. C
2. D
3. A

Page 89 • KEY WORDS
A.
1. patterns   4. moth
2. habitats   5. insect
3. prey   6. camouflage
B.
7. B   9. A
8. D   10. C

Page 90 • ACADEMIC WORDS
A.
1. l p e l (environment) b l p r a t
2. d g i l (enable) e s v o n m e n t l
B.
3. TRUE   5. TRUE
4. FALSE   6. TRUE
C.
7. Answers will vary. 8. Answers will vary.

Page 91 • WORD STUDY
1. toothbrush   5. rainbow
2. grasshopper   6. earthworm
3. lawnmower   7. backyard
4. lakehouse   8. sunset

Page 92 • COMPREHENSION
1. a walking stick
2. to keep safe and catch prey
3. camouflage
4. They could be seen and eaten by other animals.
5. **Possible response:** They can't hide. They may die.

Page 93 • READER'S COMPANION
Possible responses
Use What You Know
1. Some animals eat other animals. 2. Cats like to sleep.
Reading Strategy
C–Arctic foxes live where the weather is very cold. E– In winter, they are white. C– A tawny frogmouth is a bird. It sits very still in a tree. E– It waits for prey to come near. Then it pounces! C– Patterns help this moth stay safe. Look at the big spots on the moth's wings. They look like a large animal's eyes. E– Predators stay away from this insect.
Comprehension Check
A tawny frogmouth is a bird.

Page 94
Possible responses
Use the Strategy
The foxes turn white in winter so they can camouflage in the snow.
Retell It!
You may think that a tiger is too big to hide. But the Bengal tiger's stripes help it hide in the forest.
Reader's Response
I would like to know how the tawny frogmouth got its name.

Page 95 • LEARNING STRATEGIES
Jarrett Goes to School
Cause: Jarrett's bike got a flat tire.
Effect: Jarrett was late for school.
Allison and Rusty
Cause: Rusty ran away. Allison called his name.
Effect: Rusty came back.

Page 96 • GRAMMAR
1. big
2. tall
3. three
4. green
5. round
6. quickly
7. softly
8. quietly
9. loudly

Page 97 • SPELLING
1. newspaper
2. crosswalk
3. something
4. scarecrow
5. airplane
6. sunrise
7. fingernail
8. daydream

Writing Activity
Possible response: It was sunrise as I walked on the sidewalk. I was reading the newspaper. It was a pretty day.

Page 98 • WRITING
1. A
2. C
3. B

Page 99 • KEY WORDS
A.
1. butterfly
2. caterpillar, chrysalis
3. tadpole
4. leaves
5. hatch

B.
6. twsdfnte leaf mn
7. pe butterfly pe
8. ca caterpillar eg
9. serfute tadpole
10. d hatch jrtionhx

Page 100 • ACADEMIC WORDS
A.
1. l p e l e n l n m e n transform
2. e n occurs l a p d r i c o n m e h

B.
3. TRUE
4. FALSE
5. FALSE
6. FALSE
7. TRUE

C.
8. Answers will vary. 9. Answers will vary.

Page 101 • PHONICS
A.
1. circle *ch*
2. circle *sh*
3. circle *th*
4. circle *ch*
5. circle *th*

B.
6. shoe
7. another
8. thanks
9. touch
10. rush

Page 102 • COMPREHENSION
1. on a leaf
2. in the water
3. can swim in the water and hop on land
4. **Possible response:** They develop from eggs. They are both vulnerable to enemies.
5. Caterpillars spin a cocoon and develop inside of it. Tadpoles develop in the water.

Page 103 • READER'S COMPANION
Possible Responses
Use What You Know
1. ant, bee
Reading Strategy
1. A butterfly must find a place to lay eggs. 2. A tiny caterpillar crawls out. 3. The caterpillar builds a chrysalis around itself. 4. Then, the butterfly breaks out of the chrysalis.
Comprehension Check
Circle *A leaf is a good place.*

Page 104
Use the Strategy
It builds a chrysalis around itself.
Retell It!
The butterfly starts off as a caterpillar. The caterpillar builds a chrysalis around itself. Changes happen inside the chrysalis. The caterpillar turns into a butterfly and breaks out of the chrysalis.
Reader's Response
I have seen butterflies that are all different colors. Some are very big and some are very small. Some butterflies are yellow, red, blue, and brown.

Page 105 • LEARNING STRATEGIES
Life Cycle of a Robin
2
1
4
3
Life Cycle of a Frog
3
1
4
2

Page 106 • GRAMMAR
1. early
2. soon
3. later
4. Now
5. We will have a math test later.
6. Soon our bus will be here.

Page 107 • SPELLING
1. hutch
2. batch
3. Pitch
4. match
5. watch
6. ditch
7. watch
8. sketch

Writing Activity
Possible response: Sam caught a big fish in the ditch by his house. He let it go and watched it swim away.

Page 108 • WRITING
1. C
2. B
3. B

Pages 109–110 • REVIEW
1. D
2. **Possible response:** The lions try to eat some of the zebras, and the zebras try to stay away from the lions.
3. Cause: The rabbit must hide from predators. Effect: It hides in leaves on the ground.
4. A
5. C
6. A tadpole lives in the water.
7. B
8. Both frogs and butterflies come out of eggs.

Page 111–112 • WRITING WORKSHOP
1. B
2. C
3. B
4. D
5. A

Page 115 • TEST PREPARATION
1. mammal
2. strong
3. claws

Page 116
1. they want to protect themselves
2. to see wild animals

Unit 4

Page 117 • KEY WORDS
A.
1. volunteers
2. donate
3. bicycles
4. helmets

B.
5. donate: give something to a person or group that needs help
6. bicycles: vehicles with two wheels that you sit on and ride by moving your legs
7. helmets: hard hats that protect heads
8. volunteers: people who help others without being paid

Page 118 • ACADEMIC WORDS
A.
1. k m z benefits g h w
2. d b normally t s a f e

B.
3. normally
4. benefit
5. benefit
6. normally

C.

7. Answers will vary.
8. Answers will vary.

Page 119 • WORD STUDY

A.

1. loaded
2. fixed
3. repaired
4. hunted
5. learned

B.

6. The spaceship landed on the moon.
7. I stacked the cups on the shelf.
8. Did you like how the movie ended?
9. We painted pictures in art class.
10. Jenna looked out the window.

Page 120 • COMPREHENSION

1. They are thrown away.
2. donate them
3. They are fixed and sent to people in other countries.
4. Helmets will keep the bike riders safe.
5. They want to help others.

Page 121 • READER'S COMPANION
Possible responses
Use What You Know

1. my driveway 2. the sidewalk
Reading Strategy
his own bike broke.
He would learn how to fix it himself.
Comprehension Check
children who did not have families

Page 122
Possible responses
Use the Strategy
Joshua solved the problem of what to do with old bikes.
Retell It!
When I was twelve, my bike broke. I decided to try to fix it myself. I did a good job. Soon my neighbors were bringing me old bikes to fix. I gave the bikes to children who did not have bicycles.
Reader's Response
I would like to give books to children who don't have them.

Page 123 • LEARNING STRATEGIES

Problem	Solution
Jamie wants a new bike.	His sister will give him her old bike.
The sister's bike has a flat tire.	Jamie uses Kara's tire pump to fix the tire.

Page 124 • GRAMMAR

1. need to study
2. want to play
3. like to visit
4. loves to bake
5. wants to fix

6. I need to study for the test.
7. I want to ride my bicycle today.

Page 125 • SPELLING

1. mixes
2. wishes
3. reaches
4. buzzes
5. touches
6. pushes
7. guesses
8. relaxes

Writing Activity
Possible response: Andre dresses for school. He reaches up to comb his hair. He wishes he could go back to bed.

Page 126 • WRITING

1. B
2. C
3. B

Page 127 • KEY WORDS

A.

1. scientists
2. instinct
3. tool
4. lab
5. proof

B.

6. c
7. d
8. b
9. e
10. a

Page 128 • ACADEMIC WORDS

A.

1. k m z b e t h e o r y c h s a v
2. d b n a p r m e t h o d s a f e

B.

3. method
4. theory
5. theory
6. method

C.

7. Answers will vary.
8. Answers will vary.

Page 129 • PHONICS

1. curved; circle ur
2. girl; circle ir
3. verb; circle er
4. shirt; circle ir
5. first; circle ir
6. herd; circle er
7. burn; circle ur
8. turn; circle ur

Page 130 • COMPREHENSION

1. caw
2. to learn more about them
3. clams and walnuts
4. You are born with instinct. You learn by studying.
5. They have learned to solve problems.

Page 131 • READER'S COMPANION
Possible responses
Use What You Know

1. They have wings. 2. They have beaks.
3. They like to eat.
Reading Strategy
Scientists study crows to learn more about them.
They watch what crows do in their habitat. They also study crows in labs.
Comprehension Check
crows fly over trees.
crow sit on a power line

Page 132
Possible responses
Use the Strategy
Scientists study crows to learn more about them.
Scientists watch crows in their habitats and in labs.
Retell It!
You may watch crows flying or sitting. You may hear them call. We scientists also watch crows. We watch them in their habitat. We study them in labs. We want to learn more about crows.
Reader's Response
I like to watch ants. They move in a line. Sometimes they carry bits of food. They are always busy.

Page 133 • LEARNING STRATEGIES
Possible responses
Main idea: Crows work together to take care of their babies.
Supporting Details: The crows build a nest together. The mother sits on the eggs and the father
brings her food. The father guards the babies while the mother goes to get food.

Page 134 • GRAMMAR

A.

1. ate
2. broke
3. found
4. drank
5. swam

B.

7. **Possible responses:** came; They came to school.
8. **Possible responses:** sang; We sang a song.

Page 135 • SPELLING
Possible responses

1. experiment – a scientific test to show how something will react in a particular situation
2. observe – watch something carefully
3. behavior – the way that a person or animal does or says things

Writing Activity
Dr. Drew studies frogs. She observes them in their home near a pond. She does an experiment to test their behavior. She puts out some food. She watches to see if the frogs will share.

Page 136 • WRITING

1. C
2. B
3. A

Page 137 • KEY WORDS

A.

1. robe
2. painting
3. tepee
4. quilt

B.

7. TRUE
8. FALSE
9. FALSE
10. TRUE

5. mask
6. costume

Page 138 • ACADEMIC WORDS
A.

P	Q	U	I	L	T	I	R
R	O	F	R	P	E	P	F
L	R	I	G	K	E	Y	A
V	S	Y	M	B	O	L	Y
D	A	D	K	P	E	N	M
E	Z	S	M	D	L	M	B
P	A	C	I	M	P	L	Y
M	C	O	S	T	U	M	U

B.
2. symbol
3. imply
C.
4. Answers will vary.
5. Answers will vary.

Page 139 • PHONICS
A.
1. cow   3. because
2. come   4. cut
B.
5. celebrate   7. fancy
6. circle   8. center

Page 140 • COMPREHENSION
1. Native Americans
2. moccasins
3. cornhusk dolls
4. They decorated everything they made.
5. They depended on their environment for food, clothing, and other things they needed.

Page 141 • READER'S COMPANION
1. clothing
2. costumes
3. paintings
Reading Strategy
All of the objects show what was important to the people who made them.
Comprehension Check
paintings; pottery

Page 142
Use the Strategy
Possible response: What do the objects tell us?
Retell It!
Possible response: I make everything I need. I make my own clothes and costumes for special events. I make what is important to me. The objects I make have stories to tell.
Reader's Response
Answers will vary.

Page 143 • LEARNING STRATEGIES
1. on a buffalo hunt
2. robes and teepees

Page 144 • GRAMMAR
A.
1. circle   6. underline
2. underline   7. circle
3. underline   8. underline
4. circle   9. circle
5. circle   10. underline
B.
Possible responses
11. Sue
12. Texas
13. Austin
14. Colorado

Page 145 • SPELLING
1. squeeze   4. quiet
2. quack   5. quarter
3. square   6. squeak
Writing Activity
Possible response: Once upon a time, there was a queen who loved to make quilts. She cut square pieces of beautiful cloth. Many children helped her. The work was not quiet. The children squealed with laughter as they worked.

Page 146 • WRITING
1. C   3. C
2. D

Pages 147–148 • REVIEW
1. D
2. **Possible response:** People can donate their old bikes to other people who don't have bikes.
3. **Possible response:** Bicycle Exchange gives bikes to children, so the volunteers want to be sure the children ride safely.
4. **Possible response:** Crows dropped walnuts on the street or placed them on crosswalks. Cars drove over them and cracked the shells.
5. A
6. **Possible response:** Mateo weaves a rug on a loom.
7. B

Pages 149–150 • WRITING WORKSHOP
1. D
2. C
3. A
4. C
5. B

Page 153 • TEST PREPARATION
1. The White House garden
2. Children from local schools

Page 154
1. it provided everything they needed
2. to turn or wind

Unit 5

Page 155 • KEY WORDS
A.   **B.**
1. rotates   6. craters
2. sphere   7. rotates
3. planets   8. continents
4. continents   9. sphere
5. billions   10. planets

Page 156 • ACADEMIC WORDS
A.
1. k m z b e n e f i assign w
2. d b consist of m a p l y r
B.
3. consist of   5. consist of
4. assign   6. assign
C.
7. Answers will vary.
8. Answers will vary.

Page 157 • WORD STUDY
A.   **B.**
1. B   6. old
2. D   7. short
3. C   8. fast
4. E   9. awake
5. A   10. heavy

Page 158 • COMPREHENSION
1. sphere
2. the moon
3. light and heat
4. There are too many of them and we can't see them all.
5. The sun is a star so it is made of hot gas.

Page 159 • READER'S COMPANION
Possible responses
Use What You Know
1. Earth 2. the sun 3. stars
Reading Strategy
When our side of Earth faces the sun, we have day. When our side faces away from the sun, we have night.
Comprehension Check
It is too hot.

Page 160
Possible responses
Use the Strategy
The sun is closer to Earth than any other star.
Retell It!
The sun is a star. It gives us warmth and light. The eight planets orbit around the sun.
Reader's Response
I'd like to travel to Mars and build a settlement for people to live on.

Page 161 • LEARNING STRATEGIES
1. Stars are many times bigger than Earth.
2. Stars look small because they are far away.
3. Stars are made of gas and dust.
4. Answers will vary.

Page 162 • GRAMMAR
1. C
2. A
3. B
4. From space Earth's oceans look blue and continents look brown and green.
5. The sun warms and lights Earth.

Page 163 • SPELLING
1. photographer
2. elephant
3. phone
4. alphabet
5. sphere
Writing Activity
Possible response: I took a photograph of an elephant. I teach my little sister the alphabet. May I see your phone?

Page 164 • WRITING
1. C
2. A
3. B

Page 165 • KEY WORDS
A.
1. canoe
2. rainbow
3. bark
4. handprints
B.
5. bark
6. handprints
7. rainbow
8. canoe

Page 166 • ACADEMIC WORDS
A.
1. k m z b (t r a d i t i o n a l) s t l
2. d (p h e n o m e n o n) l y r m e n
B.
3. traditional
4. phenomenon
5. phenomenon
6. traditional
C.
7. Answers will vary.
8. Answers will vary.

Page 167 • WORD STUDY
1. soft back part of a leg
2. inside surface of the hand
3. something you hear
4. part of some plants where the grains grow

Page 168 • COMPREHENSION
1. on Earth
2. the Moon
3. into the sky
4. the Moon
5. to explain natural phenomenon

Page 169 • READER'S COMPANION
Possible responses
Use What You Know
craters
Reading Strategy
She loved them very much. She wanted them to live forever. So she sent her children into the sky.
Genre
The Sun and the Moon.

Page 170
Possible responses
Use the Strategy
The son became the sun and the daughter became the moon. The daughter was touched on her cheek by Earth Mother; the son was not touched by Earth Mother.
Retell It!
My mother wanted us to live forever. So she sent my brother to live in the sky as the sun and she sent me to live in the sky as the moon.
Reader's Response
Answers will vary.

Page 171 • LEARNING STRATEGIES
1. Venus and Mars are both planets. They both have mountains, volcanoes, and craters.
2. Venus is hot and Mars is cold. Mars has ice, but Venus has no water at all. Venus is larger than Mars.

Page 172 • GRAMMAR
1. am
2. is
3. are
4. are
5. She will climb to the top of the tree.
6. We will study the moon and the planets.

Page 173 • SPELLING
1. to
2. two
3. Two
4. too
5. too
Writing Activity
Possible response
There were two puppies at my house. I love puppies. My sister loves puppies, too. I want to bring the puppies to school to show my friends.

Page 174 • WRITING
1. A
2. D
3. D

Page 175 • KEY WORDS
A.
1. spacewalks
2. flight
3. observe
4. space shuttle
5. satellite
B.
6. D
7. B
8. C
9. E
10. A

Page 176 • ACADEMIC WORDS
A.
1. significant
2. immigrate
3. significant
4. immigrate
B.
5. immigrate
6. a significant

Page 177 • PHONICS
1. far
2. porch; story
3. sports; are hard
4. started; bark
5. marching; performed
6. orbit
7. scored; before
8. store; dark
9. morning; horses; barn
10. cars; horns

Page 178 • COMPREHENSION
1. an astronaut
2. science and reading
3. a scientist
4. That is the language of the space program.
5. Possible answers: He learned science. He got into the space program. It helped him later in life.

Pages 179 • READER'S COMPANION
Use What You Know
Possible responses: 1. go to college.
2. become a teacher
Reading Strategy
In 1980, Franklin was chosen to become an astronaut. Franklin went on more space flights than anyone had ever done before. He says that we must take care of Earth.
Comprehension Check
the sight of Earth from outer space

Page 180
Possible responses
Use the Strategy
Franklin was chosen to be an astronaut. He studied six years before his first flight. Then he went on six more flights, doing experiments, and making spacewalks.
Retell It!
Earth looks beautiful from space. We must take care of our home.
Reader's Response
Franklin worked hard to achieve his goals. He will inspire other people to take care of Earth.

Page 181 • LEARNING STRATEGIES
Possible response: Mars is the fourth planet from our sun. A robot helps us study Mars. Some scientists think that there are living things on Mars.

Page 182 • GRAMMAR
1. because
2. because
3. so
4. because
5. so
6. so

Page 183 • SPELLING

1. sight
2. lightning
3. bright

4. night
5. right

Writing Activity

Possible response: One night, there was a bright moon. It looked like daylight. My family and I went outside. We played catch! It was a beautiful sight.

Page 184 • WRITING

1. C
2. A

Pages 185–186 • REVIEW

1. B
2. **Possible response:** Constellations are groups of stars that look like a picture. People named constellations for things they knew, such as animals.
3. C
4. B
5. **Possible response:** The myth tells how the moon appears, gets larger, then disappears over and over. The selection explains that the moon is our nearest neighbor, that it has no air, no water, and no living things. Twelve astronauts have walked on the moon.
6. **Possible response:** Franklin was excited about Sputnik. He decided to be an astronaut when he was seven years old. He was a good student and curious about the world. He liked to repair things.
7. **Possible response:** Franklin was good at fixing things because he liked to repair things as a boy.

Page 187–188 • WRITING WORKSHOP

1. A
2. B
3. A

4. C
5. D

Page 191 • TEST PREPARATION

1. Apollo 11
2. two
3. The day man first landed on the moon

Page 192

1. space traveler
2. monkeys are like people

Unit 6

Page 193 • KEY WORDS

A.
1. festival
2. supplies
3. advertise
4. annual
5. schedule

B.
6. schedule
7. annual
8. festival
9. advertise
10. supplies

Page 194 • ACADEMIC WORDS

A.
1. k(annual)calitnw
2. dbcon(participate)

B.
3. participate
4. participate

5. annual
6. annual

C.
7. Answers will vary. 8. Answers will vary.

Page 195 • PHONICS

1. down, ground
2. Cows, owls
3. Wow, mouse
4. scout, brown
5. clown, frowning

6. followed, crowd
7. clouds, round
8. found, couch
9. loud, sound
10. south, town

Page 196 • COMPREHENSION

1. Red Tree
2. Ms. Tan
3. art supplies
4. **Possible response:** so she wouldn't have to spend her own money; art supplies are expensive
5. **Possible response:** to attract as many people as possible; because it is for many different ages

Page 197 • READER'S COMPANION

Possible responses
Use What You Know
1. drawing
2. paper flowers
Reading Strategy
Summer Arts Festival
Comprehension Check
take art classes, go to demonstration to learn how to make pottery or a collage

Page 198

Possible responses
Use the Strategy
The author's purpose is to tell about the Summer Arts Festival.
Retell It!
The Summer Arts Festival is held each year in Red Tree. There are art classes for people of all ages. You can watch people make pottery and collages.
Reader's Response
I would like to learn more about making pottery. My grandmother was a potter.

Page 199 • LEARNING STRATEGIES

1. The author's purpose is to inform and persuade.
2. **Possible response:** The author tells his grandmother when and where the art show is. He tries to persuade her to come by telling her he has a painting of her cat in the show.

Page 200 • GRAMMAR

1. Dear Aunt Jane,
2. Sunday, February 7

3. Your friend, John Malloy
4. St. Louis, MO 63117
5. Friday, May 15
6. Sincerely, Mona Tyler
7. Mom bought bananas, grapes, mangos, and oranges at the fruit stand.
8. We saw lions, monkeys, zebras, and giraffes at the zoo.

Page 201 • SPELLING

1. school
2. schooner
3. scheme

4. schedule
5. scholar

Writing Activity
Possible response

Time	Activity
8:30	Greeting
8:45–9:30	Reading
9:30–10	Art
10–10:45	Math
10:45–11:30	Science

Page 202 • WRITING

Answers will vary.

Page 203 • KEY WORDS

A.
1. scissors
2. stapler
3. buttons
4. yarn
5. puppets

B.
6. puppets
7. yarn
8. scissors
9. stapler
10. buttons

Page 204 • ACADEMIC WORDS

A.
1. kp(required)etting
2. dbconpar(reverse)t

B.
3. reverse
4. required

5. reverse
6. required

C.
7. Answers will vary.
8. Answers will vary.

Page 205 • PHONICS

A.
1. party
2. city
3. community
4. silly
5. happy

B.
6. you
7. yet
8. yard
9. yell
10. yo-yo

Page 206 • COMPREHENSION

1. thousands of years
2. gather supplies
3. put on a show, tell a story
4. So the puppets will turn out.
5. **Possible response** You can make it look any way you want. You can use the puppet to create stories and shows.

Page 207 • READER'S COMPANION
Possible responses
Use What You Know
1. buttons 2. colored paper
Reading Strategy
I can make a puppet with these things.
Comprehension Check
yarn, colored paper

Page 208
Possible responses
Use the Strategy
My purpose is to find out what supplies I need to make a puppet.
Retell It!
To make a puppet, gather together white paper plates, scissors, a stapler, glue, yarn, buttons, colored paper, and crayons, markers, or paint.
Reader's Response
Possible response: I would have my puppet tell jokes to the audience.

Page 209 • LEARNING STRATEGIES
1. to learn how to do something
2. to learn new facts or ideas
3. to enjoy
4. to learn new facts or ideas

Page 210 • GRAMMAR
A.
1. Drink your orange juice.
3. Look at your book.
5. Help your grandmother.
6. Don't touch the birthday cake.
B.
7. Clear the table and wash the dishes.
8. Do not eat cookies before dinner.

Page 211 • SPELLING
1. gems   4. gentle
2. magic   5. giants
3. giraffe
Writing Activity
Possible response: I made friends with a magic giraffe. She could be a giant. She could also be tiny. She was always gentle.

Page 212 • WRITING
Answers will vary.

Page 213 • KEY WORDS
A.   B.
1. booth   6. instruments
2. instruments   7. artists

3. artists   8. booth
4. musicians   9. perform
5. perform   10. musicians

Page 214 • ACADEMIC WORDS
A.
1. a l t e r n a t i v e c a l i t n w
2. d b c o n g o a l r e a n a t e
B.
3. goal   5. alternative
4. goal   6. alternative
C.
7. Answers will vary.
8. Answers will vary.

Page 215 • WORD STUDY

Two Syllables	music, trumpet, quartet
Three Syllables	festival, microphone, popular
Four Syllables	traditional, dictionary, complicated

Page 216 • COMPREHENSION
1. in Tennessee
2. four days
3. summer
4. So they can sing before large crowds. They want to sell their CDs.
5. **Possible response:** There are events and activities for all ages, and there is new music every year.

Page 217 • READER'S COMPANION
Use What You Know
Possible responses: jazz, rock, country
Reading Strategy
Country music also began in the South.
Comprehension Check
both jazz and country music

Page 218
Use the Strategy
Possible answers: Since they play many kinds of music, it should appeal to everyone.
Retell It!
Possible answers: I love to perform at the Bonnaroo Music and Arts Festival. There are eight different stages and 130 bands. I can meet my fans and sign autographs. There are other fun things to do. I take my family because there are games for kids.
Reader's Response
Answers will vary.

Page 219 • LEARNING STRATEGIES
1. They play bluegrass music at the festival. Bluegrass music is played on the banjo.
2. He wants to play bluegrass music some day.

Page 220 • GRAMMAR
A.
1. Mom said, "We must go to bed."
2. Sonia asked Dad, "Will you help me?"
3. "I read that book," Mike said.
4. Kim said, "That is my dog."
B.
5. Jason said, "Math is my favorite subject."
6. Sharon said, "I ate three cupcakes."

Page 221 • SPELLING
1. scissors
2. microphone
3. beautiful
4. dancer
5. concert
Writing Activity
although
balloon
enough
know
their

Page 222 • WRITING
Answers will vary.

Page 223–224 • REVIEW
1. D
2. C
3. Annual means it happens once each year.
4. B
5. **Possible response:** You could add yarn to give it hair.
6. **Possible responses:** make crafts; learn to grow food; ride the ferris wheel; watch an outdoor movie
7. Answers will vary.

Page 225–226 • WRITING WORKSHOP
1. C   4. B
2. B   5. C
3. A

Page 229 • TEST PREPARATION
1. ingredients   3. snacks
2. fruit

Page 230
1. art show
2. because an art festival is a big project

LETTERS HOME

Dear Family,

For the next few weeks, our class will be studying about communities. We will talk about what children do in different communities and why individuals are important to their communities. We will also talk about how families are like communities.

You can help your child learn more about communities. Talk to your child about the community you live in now or the community you lived in as a child. You may give information about:
- what kinds of jobs people have in the community
- how people live in the community
- where people play in the community

Also talk about things in the community that help people to live, work, and play. This will help your child understand how he or she fits into the community.

In this unit, students will play a guessing game. You can help your child by playing a similar game at home. Describe a place in your community and let your child guess where it is. Encourage your child to describe objects for you to guess about.

Students will also write an essay describing an event. To help your child, talk about events that take place in your family or community. Encourage your child to give you details about a favorite event.

At the end of this unit, your child will talk about how communities are alike and different. Your child may need to search the Internet or find other information at the school library. I am also encouraging your child to read other books about communities. Ask your child to talk to you about what he or she is doing in school and the additional books he or she is reading for the unit.

Thank you for helping us with our unit about communities.

Sincerely,

_____

Teacher

Estimada familia,

Durante las próximas semanas vamos a estudiar en clase el tema de las comunidades. Vamos a hablar de lo que hacen los niños en diferentes comunidades, cómo se parecen y por qué los individuos son importantes para sus comunidades. También vamos a hablar de cómo las familias son como las comunidades.

Usted puede ayudar a su hijo/a a aprender más acerca de las diferentes comunidades. Hable con su hijo/a acerca de la comunidad en la que viven en la actualidad, o en la que usted vivió de niño. Puede proporcionar información acerca de:
- el tipo de trabajo que la gente tiene en la comunidad
- cómo vive la gente en la comunidad
- dónde se divierte la gente en la comunidad

Hablen también de cosas de la comunidad que ayudan a la gente a vivir, trabajar, y divertirse. Esto ayudará a su hijo/a a entender cómo él/ella es parte de la comunidad.

En esta unidad los alumnos van a jugar un juego de adivinanzas. Usted puede ayudar a su hijo/a jugando un juego similar en casa. Describa un lugar en su comunidad y deje que su hijo/a adivine de qué lugar se trata. Anime a su hijo/a a que describa objetos para que usted adivine de qué se trata.

Los alumnos también van a escribir una composición describiendo un evento. Para ayudar a su hijo/a, hablen de eventos de su familia o comunidad. Anime a su hijo/a a que le dé detalles acerca de su evento favorito.

Al final de la unidad su hijo/a va a hablar de cómo se parecen y se diferencian las comunidades entre sí. Puede que su hijo/a tenga que usar Internet o que encontrar información adicional en la biblioteca de la escuela. También le estoy pidiendo a su hijo/a que lea otros libros acerca de las comunidades. Pídale a su hijo/a que le hable de los proyectos que está haciendo, así como de los libros adicionales que está leyendo para esta unidad.

Gracias por ayudarnos con nuestra unidad acerca de las comunidades.

Atentamente,

_____

Profesor/a

Dear Family,

For the next few weeks, our class will be studying about meeting challenges. We will talk about solving problems and trying new things.

You can help your child learn more about meeting challenges. Talk to your child about a person who meets challenges here in the United States or in your country of origin. You may give information about:
  • the person's background
  • what the person did to meet his or her challenges

Talk to your child about a challenge that he or she could meet. Talk about the activities your child has to do to meet these challenges. This exercise will help your child understand that people must work hard to meet challenges.

In this unit, students will perform a skit. You can help by asking your child to act out a favorite scene from one of the readings. Encourage your child to pretend to be different characters in the story.

Students will also write a story. You can help by telling stories about things that have happened to you. Ask your child to tell you a story about a personal experience. If he or she can't think of anything, ask about something funny that happened in school or something unusual that happened at lunch.

At the end of this unit, your child may work alone or with another student on a project. Your child may have to use the Internet or find other information at the school library to do this project. I am also encouraging your child to read other books about meeting challenges. Ask your child to talk to you about the projects he or she is doing and the additional books he or she is reading for this unit.

Thank you for helping us with our unit about meeting challenges.

Sincerely,

_____

Teacher

Estimada familia,

Durante las próximas semanas vamos a estudiar en clase el tema de superar desafíos. Vamos a hablar acerca de resolver problemas y tener nuevas vivencias.

Usted puede ayudar a su hijo/a a aprender a superar desafíos. Hable con su hijo/a acerca de una persona que tiene que superar desafíos aquí en los Estados Unidos o en su país de origen. Puede darle información acerca de:
- el historia de la persona
- lo que hizo esta persona para superar los desafíos

Hable con su hijo/a acerca de un desafío que él o ella ha podido superar. Hablen acerca de lo que su hijo tiene que hacer para superar esos desafíos. Este ejercicio va a ayudar a su hijo/a a entender que es necesario trabajar para superar desafíos.

En esta unidad los alumnos van a representar una breve obra teatral. Usted puede ayudar pidiéndole a su hijo/a que represente una de sus escenas favoritas de una de las lecturas. Anime a su hijo/a a que represente diferentes personajes de la historia.

Los alumnos también van a escribir una historia. Usted puede ayudar contándole historias a su hijo/a acerca de cosas que le pasaron a usted. Pídale a su hijo/a que le cuente una historia acerca de una experiencia personal. Si no se le ocurre nada, pregúntele por algo gracioso que pasó en la escuela o de algo inusual que pasó a la hora del almuerzo.

Al final de la unidad, su hijo/a puede que tenga que trabajar solo/a o con otro alumno en un proyecto. Para completar este proyecto, puede que su hijo/a tenga que usar Internet o que encontrar información adicional en la biblioteca de la escuela. También le estoy pidiendo a su hijo/a que lea otros libros acerca de superar desafíos. Pídale a su hijo/a que le hable de los proyectos que está haciendo, así como de los libros adicionales que está leyendo para esta unidad.

Gracias por ayudarnos con nuestra unidad acerca de superar desafíos.

Atentamente,

_____

Profesor/a

Dear Family,

For the next few weeks, our class will be studying about animals at home. We will talk about how animals grow, about their habitats, and about why some animals behave the way they do.

You can help your child learn more about animals at home. Talk to your child about animals in the United States or in your country of origin. Also talk to your child about animals you have or may have had in your home. Discuss some of the differences between some of the animals. How did the animals affect you? This will help your child better understand how to live with animals.

As part of this unit, students will write and recite a poem about a favorite activity or animal. You can help your child by talking about poems you like, either in English or in your native language. Ask your child to read out loud the poem he or she has written.

Students will also write a personal narrative. Talk to your child about different things he or she has done. Remind the child of classes or camps he or she has gone to, or visits or trips he or she has taken. Ask what your child learned from these events. This will help your child decide what to write about.

At the end of this unit, your child may work alone or with other students on a project. Your child may need to use the Internet or find other information at the school library to do this project. I am also encouraging your child to read other books about animals at home. Ask your child to talk about the school projects he or she is doing and the additional books he or she may be reading for this unit.

Thank you for helping us with our unit about animals at home.

Sincerely,

_____

Teacher

Estimada familia,

Durante las próximas semanas vamos a estudiar en clase el tema de los animales domésticos. Vamos a hablar de cómo crecen los animales, de sus hábitats, y por qué algunos animales se comportan del modo que lo hacen.

Usted puede ayudar a su hijo/a a aprender más acerca de los animales domésticos. Hable con su hijo/a acerca de animales de los Estados Unidos o de su país de origen. Hable también con su hijo/a acerca de animales que usted tenga o haya tenido en la casa. Hablen de algunas de las diferencias entre alguno de los animales. ¿Qué influencia tuvieron en usted los animales? Esto ayudará a su hijo/a entender lo que significa vivir con animales.

Como parte de esta unidad, los alumnos van a escribir y recitar un poema sobre una de sus actividades favoritas, o sobre uno de sus animales favoritos. Usted puede ayudar a su hijo/a hablándole de poemas que le gusten a usted, ya sea en inglés o en su lengua nativa. Pídale a su hijo/a que le lea en voz alto el poema que él/ella escribió.

Los alumnos también van a escribir una narrativa personal. Hable con su hijo de cosas que él/ella ha hecho. Recuérdele clases o campamentos a los que ha ido, o visitas o viajes a los que ha ido. Pregúntele a su hijo/a qué aprendió en esos eventos. Esto ayudará a su hijo/a a decidir acerca de qué va a escribir.

Al final de la unidad, su hijo puede que tenga que trabajar solo/a o con otro alumno en un proyecto. Para completar este proyecto, puede que su hijo/a tenga que usar Internet o que encontrar información adicional en la biblioteca de la escuela. También le estoy pidiendo a su hijo/a que lea otros libros acerca de animales domésticos. Pídale a su hijo/a que le hable de los proyectos que está haciendo, así como de los libros adicionales que está leyendo para esta unidad.

Gracias por ayudarnos con esta unidad acerca de los animales domésticos.

Atentamente,

_____

Profesor/a

Dear Family,

For the next few weeks, our class will be studying about great ideas. We will talk about great ideas that help people all over the world. We will also talk about scientists and inventors and how scientists test their great ideas.

You can help your child learn more about great ideas. Talk to your child about what life would be like without:

- people who have great ideas
- inventors, painters, builders, writers, and actors
- great ideas that changed the way we live

In this unit, students will give a presentation. You can help your child by asking about his or her talents or hobbies. What does the child like to do when not in school? Ask your child to describe what he or she likes about the hobby and ask questions about it. This will help your child be prepared for the presentation.

Students will also write an essay comparing and contrasting two people, places, or things. To help your child, ask what is the same and what is different about two things the child knows well. This will help your child notice similarities and differences.

At the end of this unit, your child may work alone or with other students on a project. Your child may need to search the Internet or find other information at the school library to do this project. I am also encouraging your child to read other books about great ideas. Ask your child to talk to you about the school projects he or she is doing and the additional books he or she is reading for this unit.

Thank you for helping us with our unit about great ideas.

Sincerely,

_____

Teacher

Estimada familia,

Durante las próximas semanas, vamos a estudiar en clase el tema de grandes ideas. Vamos a hablar de grandes ideas que ayudan a la gente. También vamos a hablar de científicos e inventores y de cómo los científicos prueban sus grandes ideas.

Usted puede ayudar a su hijo/a a aprender más acerca de grandes ideas. Hable con su hijo/a de cómo sería el mundo sin:
- gente con grandes ideas
- inventores, pintores, constructores, escritores, y actores
- grandes ideas que cambiaron nuestro modo de vida

En esta unidad los alumnos van a hacer una presentación. Usted puede ayudar a su hijo/a preguntándole acerca de sus habilidades o pasatiempos. ¿Qué le gusta hacer a su hijo/a cuando no está en la escuela? Pídale a su hijo/a que describa qué es lo que le gusta del pasatiempo y hágale preguntas al respecto. Esto ayudará a su hijo/a a prepararse para la presentación.

Los alumnos también van a escribir una composición comparando y contrastando dos personas, lugares o cosas. Para ayudar a su hijo/a, pregúntele en qué se parecen y en qué se diferencian dos cosas que él/ella conozca bien. Esto ayudará a su hijo/a a percatarse de parecidos y diferencias.

Al final de la unidad, su hijo puede que tenga que trabajar solo/a o con otro alumno en un proyecto. Para completar este proyecto, puede que su hijo/a tenga que usar Internet o que encontrar información adicional en la biblioteca de la escuela. También le estoy pidiendo a su hijo/a que lea otros libros acerca de grandes ideas. Pídale a su hijo/a que le hable de los proyectos que está haciendo, así como de los libros adicionales que está leyendo para esta unidad.

Gracias por ayudarnos con esta unidad acerca de grandes ideas.

Atentamente,

_____

Profesor/a

Dear Family,

For the next few weeks our class will be studying our neighbors in space. We will talk about stars, planets, and astronauts. We will also discuss different myths about the sun and the moon, and why the moon appears to change shape in the sky.

You can help your child learn more about our neighbors in space. Talk to your child about the Earth, the sun, the moon, stars, planets, and asteroids. You may give information about the phases of the moon and constellations.

Also talk about why we live on Earth and why we don't live on the other planets, or the sun or moon. Talk about how astronauts travel. Talk to your child about myths or stories that tell about our neighbors in space.

As part of this unit, students will write and present a TV newscast about space or space exploration. Watch a TV news story with your child and point out how the story answers the questions *Who, What, Where, When, Why,* and *How.* Encourage your child to practice the newscast at home.

Students will also write a review of a book or movie. Help your child by asking why he or she likes or dislikes a particular book or movie. Encourage the child to give detailed explanations for opinions.

At the end of this unit, your child may work alone or with other students on a project. Your child may need to search the Internet or find other information at the school library to do this project. I am also encouraging your child to read other books about neighbors in space. Ask your child to talk to you about the school projects he or she is doing and the additional books he or she is reading for this unit.

Thank you for helping us with our unit about neighbors in space.

Sincerely,

_____

Teacher

Estimada familia,

Durante las próximas semanas vamos a estudiar en clase el tema de nuestros vecinos del espacio. Vamos a hablar de las estrellas, de los planetas, y de los astronautas. También vamos a hablar de varios mitos acerca del sol y de la luna, y de por qué la luna parece cambiar de forma en el cielo.

Usted puede ayudar a su hijo/a acerca de nuestros vecinos en el espacio. Hable con su hijo/a acerca de la tierra, el sol, la luna, las estrellas, los planetas, y los asteroids. Puede darle información acerca de las fases lunares y constelaciones de estrellas.

Hablen también de por qué vivimos en la tierra y de por qué no vivimos en los otros planetas, en el sol, o en la luna. Hablen de los mitos o historias que hablan de nuestros vecinos en el espacio.

Como parte de esta unidad, los alumnos van a escribir y presentar un informativo de televisión acerca del espacio o de las exploraciones espaciales. Mire un programa de noticias en la televisión con su hijo/a y explíquele cómo el programa responde a las preguntas Quién, Qué, Dónde, Cuándo, Por Qué y Cómo. Anime a su hijo/a a practicar el programa de noticias en casa.

Los alumnos también van a escribir un reporte de un libro o de una película. Ayude a su hijo/a preguntándole por qué le gusta o no le gusta un determinado libro o película. Anime a su hijo/a a que le dé explicaciones detalladas de sus opiniones.

Al final de la unidad, su hijo/a puede que tenga que trabajar solo/a o con otro alumno en un proyecto. Para completar este proyecto, puede que su hijo/a tenga que usar Internet o que encontrar información adicional en la biblioteca de la escuela. También le estoy pidiendo a su hijo/a que lea otros libros acerca de nuestros vecinos en el espacio. Pídale a su hijo/a que le hable de los proyectos que está haciendo, así como de los libros adicionales que está leyendo para esta unidad.

Gracias por ayudarnos con esta unidad acerca de nuestros vecinos en el espacio.

Atentamente,

Profesor/a

Dear Family,

For the next few weeks, our class will be studying about arts festivals. We will talk about different forms of art and music from around the world. We will also talk about creating our own art.

You can help your child learn more about arts festivals. Talk to your child about puppets, masks, ceramics, dancing, and other forms of art. You may give information about arts:
- in the United States and in your country of origin
- that you admire

Talk to your child about a form of art in which he or she has interest. Talk about what your child would need to do to become more familiar with his or her chosen form of art. This activity will give your child a goal toward making an object that is his or hers.

In this unit, students will give a how-to presentation. To help, ask your child to explain to you how to perform a task or play a game. Encourage the child to explain the different steps in the order they need to occur.

Students will also write a research report. Assist your child by asking about his or her research plan and making sure the child has his or her research notes organized. Encourage your child to share what he or she learns from the research.

At the end of this unit, your child may work alone or with other students on a project. Your child may need to search the Internet or find other information at the school library to do this project. I am also encouraging your child to read other books about arts festivals. Ask your child to talk to you about the school projects he or she is doing and the additional books he or she is reading for this unit.

Thank you for helping us with our unit about arts festivals.

Sincerely,

_____

Teacher

Estimada familia,

Durante las próximas semanas vamos a estudiar en clase el tema de festivales de arte. Vamos a hablar de diferentes formas de arte y de música de diferentes partes del mundo. También vamos a hablar de cómo crear nuestro propio arte.

Ustede puede ayudar a su hijo/a a aprender más acerca de festivales de arte. Hable con su hijo/a de marionetas, mascaras, cerámicas, bailes, y otras manifestaciones artísticas. Puede proporcionarle información acerca del arte:
- en los Estados Unidos y en sus país de origen
- que a usted le gusta

Hable con su hijo/a acerca de una manifestación artística en la que él/ella esté interesado/a. Hablen de lo que su hijo/a necesita hacer para familiarizarse mejor con esa variedad de arte. A través de esta actividad, su hijo establecerá metas para hacer algo que sea enteramente suyo.

En esta unidad los alumnos van a hacer una presentación acerca de cómo se hace algo. Para ayudar, pídale a su hijo/a que le explique cómo hacer algo o cómo jugar un juego. Anime a su hijo a que le explique los diferentes pasos en el orden en el que ocurren.

Los alumnos también van a escribir un informe de investigación. Ayude a su hijo/a preguntándole acerca de su plan de investigación y asegúrese de que su hijo/a tiene sus notas en orden. Anime a su hijo/a a compartir con usted lo que ha aprendido durante la investigación.

Al final de la unidad, su hijo puede que tenga que trabajar solo/a o con otro alumno en un proyecto. Para completar este proyecto, puede que su hijo/a tenga que usar Internet o que encontrar información adicional en la biblioteca de la escuela. También le estoy pidiendo a su hijo/a que lea otros libros acerca de festivales de arte. Pídale a su hijo/a que le hable de los proyectos que está haciendo, así como de los libros adicionales que está leyendo para esta unidad.

Gracias por ayudarnos con esta unidad acerca de festivales de arte.

Atentamente,

_____

Profesor/a

READING SUMMARIES

READING 1: "Cool Hector"

English

This poem tells of a boy named Hector who lives in the city. Hector loves the city and visits the many community establishments. He goes to the park and fruit store. He rides the bus and sees a mail truck. He then stops for ice cream.

Spanish

Este poema trata sobre un niño llamado Héctor, que vive en la ciudad. A Héctor le encanta la ciudad y visita los diversos establecimientos comunitarios. Va al parque y a la frutería. Viaja en autobús y ve un camión de correo. Luego para a tomar un helado.

Hmong

Zaj paj huam no piav txog ib tug tub hluas hu ua Hector uas nyob hauv ib lub nroog. Hector nyiam lub nroog ntawd thiab mus xyuas ntau qhov chaw hauv nroog. Nws mus xyuas lub tshav puam thiab lub tsev muag txiv hmab txiv ntoo. Nws caij lub npav thiab pom lub tsheb uas xa ntawv. Nws txawm nres yuav kis lias noj.

READING 1: "Cool Hector"

Chinese

这首诗讲述了一位住在城市里的男孩 Hector。他热爱这座城市，并且经常光顾社区内的各种场所。他去公园及水果店。他坐公共汽车上，看到一辆邮政车。然后，他停下来买冰淇淋。

Cambodian

កំណាព្យនេះរៀបរាប់ប្រាប់ពីក្មេងប្រុសម្នាក់ឈ្មោះ៖ ហាកទ័រ ដែលរស់នៅក្នុងទីក្រុងមួយ ។ ហាកទ័រស្រឡាញ់ទីក្រុងនេះ និងទៅលេងគ្រឹះស្ថានសហគមន៍ជាច្រើន ។ វាទៅកាន់សួនឧទ្យាន និងហាងលក់ផ្លិញ ។ វាជិះរថយន្តក្រុង និងមើលរថយន្តដឹកសំបុត្រ ។ បន្ទាប់មកវាឈប់ញ៉ាំការ៉េម ។

Vietnamese

Bài thơ này kể về một cậu bé tên là Hector sống ở thành phố. Hector yêu thành phố và đến thăm nhiều nơi trong cộng đồng. Cậu đến công viên và tiệm bán trái cây. Cậu đi xe buýt và nhìn thấy một xe chở thư. Sau đó cậu dừng lại để mua kem.

READING 2: "Making Friends"

English

This reading tells about a classroom of children from all over the world. The teacher has them show each other something fun. Hana and Carlos are sad because they don't know anyone yet. Hana is from Japan and Carlos is from Mexico. At the end, Hana teaches Carlos origami and Carlos teaches Hana to cook a dessert. They are both happy.

Spanish

Este texto trata sobre un aula de niños de todo el mundo. El maestro les pide que compartan algo divertido. Hana y Carlos están tristes porque todavía no conocen a nadie. Hana es de Japón y Carlos de México. Al final, Hana le enseña origami a Carlos y Carlos le enseña a Hana a cocinar un postre. Ambos están felices.

Hmong

Zaj no piav txog ib chav kawm ntawv rau cov me nyuam uas nyob thoob plaws ntiaj teb no. Tus xib hwb qhia ntawv hais kom lawv ib leeg qhia ib leeg txog tej yam uas lom zem ua. Hana thiab Carlos tu siab rau qhov nkawd tseem tsis tau paub leej twg li. Hana tuaj tim Nyij Pooj teb tuaj thiab Carlos tuaj ntawm Mev teb tuaj. Thaum kawg ces, Hana qhia Carlos txog txoj kev tais ntawv ua tsiaj txhu thiab Carlos qhia Hana ua ib qho khoom qab zib. Nkawd ob leeg zoo siab lawm.

READING 2: "Making Friends"

Chinese

本文讲述了一个由来自世界各地的孩子们组成的班级。老师让孩子们彼此展示一样有趣的事物。Hana 和 Carlos 却闷闷不乐，因为他们还不认识班上的同学。Hana 来自日本，Carlos 来自墨西哥。最后，Hana 教会了 Carlos 如何做折纸，Carlos 则教会了 Hana 如何做甜点。他们两人都非常开心。

Cambodian

អំណាននេះរៀបរាប់ប្រាប់ពីថ្នាក់រៀនមួយដែលមានកុមារមកពីជុំវិញពិភពលោក ។ គ្រូបង្រៀនបានឱ្យពួកគេរៀបរាប់រឿងកំប្លែងប្រាប់គ្នាទៅវិញទៅមក ។ ហាណា និងកាឡូស មិនសប្បាយចិត្ត ព្រោះពួកគេមិនដឹងរឿង ។ ហាណា មកពីប្រទេសជប៉ុន ហើយកាឡូសមកពីប្រទេស មិុចស៊ីកូ ។ ទីបំផុត ហាណា បង្រៀនកាឡូសពីរបៀបបត់ក្រដាសជារូបផ្សេងៗ ហើយកាឡូសបង្រៀនហាណាពីរបៀប ធ្វើបង្អែម ។ ពួកគេទាំងពីរនាក់សប្បាយរីករាយណាស់ ។

Vietnamese

Bài viết này kể về một lớp học gồm học sinh đến từ khắp nơi trên thế giới. Thầy giáo yêu cầu các em chỉ cho nhau xem một điều thú vị nào đó. Hana và Carlos buồn vì các em chưa quen ai cả. Hana đến từ Nhật Bản và Carlos đến từ Mexico. Cuối cùng, Hana dạy Carlos cách xếp giấy và Carlos dạy Hana cách nấu món tráng miệng. Cả hai em đều vui vẻ.

READING 3: "My Family"

English

This reading tells of a large family that loves to celebrate special occasions. They have birthday parties, barbecues, or just plain house parties. They eat lots of food, make noise, and have fun.

Spanish

Este texto trata sobre una gran familia a la que le encanta celebrar ocasiones especiales. Festejan cumpleaños, organizan barbacoas o simples fiestas en casa. Comen mucho, hacen ruido y se divierten.

Hmong

Zaj no piav txog ib tse neeg loj loj uas nyiam ua koob tsheej nco txog tej yam tshwj xeeb. Lawv muaj kev lom zem thaum muaj hnub yug, ci nqaij, los sis muaj chaw ua si hauv tsev xwb. Lawv nyiam noj mov ntau, ua vij ua voog, thiab muaj kev lom zem.

READING 3: "My Family"

Chinese

本文讲述了一个喜欢庆祝特别场合的大家庭的故事。他们经常举办生日聚会、烧烤或普通的家庭聚会。他们会吃许多好吃的东西，一起热热闹闹地度过欢乐时光。

Cambodian

អំណាននេះរៀបរាប់ប្រាប់ពីគ្រួសារដ៏ធំមួយ ដែលចូលចិត្តរៀបចំពិធីពិសេសៗ ។ ពួកគេមានពិធីបុណ្យខួបកំណើត ការអាំងសាច់ ឬពិធី នៅផ្ទះធម្មតា ។ ពួកគេបរិភោគអាហារច្រើន មានភាពអ៊ូអរ និងសប្បាយរីករាយ ។

Vietnamese

Bài viết này kể về một gia đình đông người thích tổ chức ăn mừng vào các ngày lễ đặc biệt. Họ tổ chức những bữa tiệc sinh nhật, tiệc thịt nướng ngoài trời, hay chỉ là bữa tiệc trong nhà đơn giản. Họ ăn nhiều thức ăn, cười đùa và rất vui vẻ.

READING 1: "The Rabbit and the Lion"

English

This reading is about a rabbit and a lion. The lion catches the rabbit and tries to eat him. The lion tells the rabbit that he is the king of the forest. The sly rabbit tricks the lion by telling him that his reflection in the well is the king. The lion believes that his reflection is that of the king. The lion jumps in the well to attack the reflection. The rabbit has outsmarted the lion.

Spanish

Este texto trata sobre un conejo y un león. El león atrapa al conejo e intenta comérselo. El león le dice al conejo que él es el rey del bosque. El astuto conejo engaña al león, al convencerlo de que su reflejo en el agua es el rey. El león cree que su reflejo es el del rey. El león salta al agua para atacar a su reflejo. El conejo fue más listo que el león.

Hmong

Zaj no piav txog ib tug luav thiab ib tug tsov ntxhuav. Tus tsov ntxhuav txhom tau tus luav thiab yuav muab noj. Tus tsov ntxhuav qhia tus luav tias nws yog tus vaj ntxwv rau hav zoov. Tus luav ntxias tau tsov ntxhuav tias nws tus duab uas nws pom hauv lub qhov dej yog tus vaj ntxwv thiab. Tus tsov ntxhuav xav tias nws tus duab ntawd yog vaj ntxwv tiag. Tus tsov ntxuav dhia mus hauv lub qhov dej yuav tom tus tsov ntxhuav hauv. Tus luav thiaj dim tau tsov ntxhuav.

READING 1: "The Rabbit and the Lion"

Chinese

本文讲述了一只兔子和一头狮子的故事。狮子抓住了兔子，要吃掉他。还对他说自己是森林之王。聪明的兔子骗狮子说：井里的倒影才是森林之王。狮子信以为真，以为自己的倒影才是森林之王。他跳入井中攻击那个倒影。兔子以自己的智慧战胜了狮子。

Cambodian

អំណានទេះរៀបរាប់ប្រាប់ពីទន្សាយ និងតោ ។ តោចាប់បានទន្សាយ ហើយឃ្យាយាមស៊ីទន្សាយ ។ តោប្រាប់ទន្សាយថា ខ្លួនជាស្ដេចព្រៃ។ ទន្សាយដ៏វាងវៃបោកបញ្ឆោតដោយប្រាប់តោថា ស្រមោលឆ្លុះរបស់តោនៅក្នុងអណ្ដូងគឺជាស្ដេច ។ តោជឿថា ស្រមោលឆ្លុះរបស់ខ្លួន គឺជាស្ដេច ។ តោលោតទៅក្នុងអណ្ដូងដើម្បីវាយជាមួយស្រមោលឆ្លុះនោះ ។ ទន្សាយមានប្រាជ្ញាខ្ពស់ជាងតោ ។

Vietnamese

Bài viết này kể về một con thỏ và một con sư tử. Sư tử bắt được thỏ và cố ăn thịt chú thỏ. Sư tử bảo thỏ nó là chúa tể của khu rừng. Chú thỏ láu lỉnh lừa sư tử bằng cách bảo sư tử rằng hình phản chiếu của nó trong giếng mới chính là chúa tể. Sư tử tin hình phản chiếu của nó là chúa tể. Sư tử nhảy vào giếng để tấn công hình phản chiếu đó. Vậy là thỏ đã lừa được sư tử.

READING 2: "The Contest"

English

In this reading the main characters are the North Wind and the Sun. The North Wind is bored and decides to challenge the Sun. The North Wind sees a lady wearing a hat and tells the sun that he will be able to make the lady take off her hat first. The North Wind starts to blow, but the lady holds her hat in place. When it's the suns turn, he shines brightly and the lady takes off her hat. The lady then fans herself with her hat. The North Wind then makes a small breeze. At the end of the reading, the North Wind understands that both he and the Sun have important jobs.

Spanish

En este texto, los personajes principales son el Viento norte y el Sol. El Viento norte está aburrido y decide desafiar al Sol. El Viento norte ve a una señora con sombrero y le dice al Sol que él será el primero en hacer que la señora se quite el sombrero. El Viento norte comienza a soplar, pero la señora se sostiene el sombrero puesto. Cuando le toca su turno, el Sol brilla intensamente y la señora se quita el sombrero. La señora se abanica con el sombrero. Luego, el Viento norte sopla una brisa leve. Al final del texto, el Viento norte comprende que tanto él como el Sol tienen tareas importantes.

Hmong

Nyob hauv zaj no ob tug uas tseem ceeb yog Qhov Cua Pem Qaum Teb thiab lub Hnub. Qhov Cua Pem Qaum Teb tsis muaj kev lom zem ces nws hais kom Hnub nrog nws sib xeem. Qhov Cua Pem Qaum Teb pom ib tug poj niam uas ntoo kaus mom thiab qhia lub hnub tias nws txawj ua rau tus poj niam hle kaus mom ua ntej lub hnub yuav ua kom nws hle. Qhov Cua Pem Qaum Teb pib tshuab, tabsis tus poj niam tuav rawv nws lub kaus mom xwb. Thaum txog lub hnub thib, nws ci ntsa iab thiab tus poj niam txawm hle nws lub kaus mom. Ces tus poj niam siv lub kaus mom ntxuaj nws lub ntej muag. Ces Qhov Cua Pem Qaum Teb pib tshuab dua. Thaum xaus zaj dab neeg no, Qhov Cua Pem Qaum Teb to taub tias nws thiab lub Hnub ob leeg puav leej muaj hauj lwm tseem ceeb.

READING 2: "The Contest"

Chinese

这篇故事的主人公是北风和太阳。北风感到无聊，便决定挑战太阳。北风看见一位戴着帽子的女士，便对太阳说他可以先让那位女士摘下帽子。北风开始咆哮，但那位女士却抓着帽子不让它脱落。轮到太阳的时候，太阳放射出灿烂温暖的阳光，没一会儿，那位女士就把帽子摘了下来。然后，她煽动着帽子来乘凉。这时，北风刮起一阵微风。故事到最后，北风终于明白：自己和太阳都扮演着不同的重要角色。

Cambodian

នៅក្នុងអំណាននេះ គូអង្គសំខាន់គឺ ខ្យល់ទិសខាងជើង និងព្រះអាទិត្យ ។ ខ្យល់ទិសខាងជើងធុញទ្រាន់ ហើយសម្រេចប្រកួតជាមួយ ព្រះអាទិត្យ ។ ខ្យល់ទិសខាងជើង ឃើញនារីម្នាក់ពាក់មួក ហើយប្រាប់ព្រះអាទិត្យថា វានឹងអាចធ្វើឱ្យនារីនោះ ដោះមួកខ្លួនចេញមុន ។ ខ្យល់ទិសខាងជើងចាប់ផ្តើមបក់ តែនារីនោះនៅប់មួកខាងជាប់ ។ ដល់ពេលព្រះអាទិត្យម្តង ព្រះអាទិត្យបញ្ចេញពន្លឺខ្លាំង ហើយនារីនោះដោះ មួកនាងចេញ ។ បន្ទាប់មក នារីនោះបក់ខ្លួនឯងដោយមួករបស់នាង ។ ក្រោយមកទៀត ខ្យល់ទិសខាងជើង បានបក្ខើតខ្យល់រំភើយ ។ នៅចុងបញ្ចប់នៃអំណាននេះ ខ្យល់ទិសខាងជើងយល់ថា ទាំងខ្លួន និងព្រះអាទិត្យ មានការងារសំខាន់ដូចគ្នា ។

Vietnamese

Trong bài viết này, nhân vật chính là Gió Bắc và Mặt Trời. Gió Bắc đang buồn chán và quyết định thách thức Mặt Trời. Gió Bắc nhìn thấy một phụ nữ đang đội mũ và bảo mặt trời rằng nó có thể làm cho người phụ nữ này bỏ mũ ra trước. Gió Bắc bắt đầu thổi nhưng bà ta vẫn giữ được mũ trên đầu. Khi đến lượt mặt trời, nó chiếu sáng và bà ta phải bỏ mũ ra. Sau đó bà lấy chiếc mũ quạt cho mình. Rồi gió Bắc thổi một luồng gió nhẹ. Vào cuối bài viết, Gió Bắc hiểu rằng cả nó và Mặt Trời đều có những công việc quan trọng.

READING 3: "Sharing a Garden"

English

This reading is about creating a community garden. It describes how the neighbors plan the garden and share the chores. The reading ends with a letter sent out to all the people in the neighborhood, inviting everyone to be a part of the community garden.

Spanish

Esta lectura trata sobre la creación de un huerto comunitario. Describe la manera en que los vecinos planifican el huerto y se dividen las tareas. La lectura finaliza con una carta que se envía a todas las personas del vecindario, donde se las invita a participar en el huerto comunitario.

Hmong

Zaj no hais txog txoj kev tsim ib lub vaj hauv zej zog. Zaj no piav txog cov neeg zej zog uas npaj ua ib lub vaj thiab txhua leej txhua tus pab ua tej dej num. Thaum zaj no tag lawv xa ib tsab ntawv rau tag nrho cov neeg hauv zej zog, thov caw txhua tus los pab tu lub vaj hauv lub zos ntawd.

READING 3: "Sharing a Garden"

Chinese

这篇读物讲述一个建造社区花园的故事。它描述了邻居们如何制定花园的规划并共同分担杂务。这篇读物以一封寄给附近居民的信结束，邀请每一个人做社区花园的一分子。

Cambodian

អំណាននេះ គឺអំពីការបង្កើតសួនក្នុងសហគមន៍មួយ ។ អំណានពណ៌នាអំពីរបៀបដែលអ្នកជិតខាងទាំងឡាយដាំសួន និងចែករំលែកការងារ ។ អំណានបញ្ចប់ដោយមានលិខិតមួយផ្ញើទៅកាន់ប្រជាជនទាំងអស់ក្នុងសង្កាត់ ដោយអញ្ជើញ ម្នាក់ៗ ឱ្យធ្វើជាផ្នែកមួយនៃសួនសហគមន៍ ។

Vietnamese

Bài đọc này nói về việc lập ra một khu vườn cộng đồng. Bài đọc mô tả cách thức những người láng giềng hoạch định cho khu vườn và chia xẻ những việc cần làm. Bài đọc chấm dứt bằng một lá thư gửi cho tất cả mọi người trong khu xóm, mời tất cả mọi người tham gia vào khu vườn cộng đồng.

READING 1: "Animals At Home"

English

The poem "Animals at Home" tells about many different animals and their habitats. It tells us how beautiful it is to see all the different animals in their habitats. The poem "Little Allie Alligator" tells about a young alligator. She likes to rest all day on a log. Allie's father tries to wake her up. He wants her to eat supper with him. But Allie prefers to sleep. When Allie finally wakes up, she is hungry. Her father laughs and tells her she needs to find her own supper.

Spanish

El poema "Los animales en su hogar" trata sobre diversos animales y sus hábitats. Nos cuenta lo maravilloso que es observar a los distintos animales en sus hábitats. El poema "La pequeña cocodrila Coca" trata sobre una joven cocodrila a la que le gusta dormir todo el día sobre un tronco. El padre de Coca intenta despertarla porque quiere que cene con él. Pero Coca prefiere dormir. Cuando Coca finalmente se despierta, tiene hambre. Su padre se ríe y le dice que tiene que buscarse su propia cena.

Hmong

Zaj paj huam "Cov Tsiaj Txhu tej Qhov Chaw Nyob" qhia txog ntau tus tsiaj txhua thiab qhov chaw uas lawv nyob. Zaj no qhia txog qhov uas yus pom tag nrho cov tsiaj txhu nyob hauv lawv chaw nyob yog ib qho zoo nkauj heev. Zaj paj huam "Tus Me Nyuam Khej Allie" qhia txog ib tug khej hluas. Nws nyiam pw saum ib ya ntoo tas ib hnub. Allie txiv sim tsa nws sawv. Nws xav kom Allie nrog nws noj hmo. Tiamsis Allie nyiam pw xwb. Thaum Allie tsim los, nws tshaib plab. Nws txiv luag thiab qhia nws tias nws yuav tsum nrhiav dab tsi rau nws tus kheej noj.

READING 1: "Animals At Home"

Chinese

"动物在家里"这首诗谈到许多各种各样的动物以及他们各自的生活环境。它告诉我们，看到各种动物生活在适合自己的生活环境中是多么美好。"小鳄鱼艾莉"这首诗讲述了一头小鳄鱼的故事。小鳄鱼艾莉喜欢整天睡在一块原木上。艾莉的爸爸想叫醒她，让艾莉和他一起吃晚饭。可是艾莉宁愿睡觉。最后艾莉终于醒了，她饿了。爸爸大笑，说她得自己找晚饭。

Cambodian

កំណាព្យអំពី "សត្វនៅផ្ទះ" រៀបរាប់អំពីបណ្ដាសត្វខុសៗគ្នាជាច្រើន និងទីលំនៅរបស់ពួកវា ។ កំណាព្យប្រាប់យើងអំពីភាពស្រស់ស្អាតក្នុងការមើលសត្វផ្សេងៗទាំងអស់នៅក្នុងទីលំនៅរបស់ពួកវា ។ កំណាព្យអំពី "ក្រពើឈ្មោះអាលីតូច" រៀបរាប់អំពីក្រពើតូចមួយ ។ វាចូលចិត្តដេករាល់ថ្ងៃនៅលើគល់ឈើមួយ ។ ឪពុករបស់អាលី ព្យាយាមដាស់វាឱ្យក្រោកឡើង ។ គាត់ចង់ឱ្យវាស៊ីអាហារពេលយប់ជាមួយគាត់ ។ តែអាលីចូលចិត្តដេកជាង ។ ចុងក្រោយពេលដែលអាលីដឹងខ្លួនឡើង វាឃ្លាន ។ ឪពុកវាសើច ហើយប្រាប់វាថា វាត្រូវតែស្វែងរកអាហារពេលយប់ដោយខ្លួនវាផ្ទាល់ ។

Vietnamese

Bài thơ "Animals at Home" kể về nhiều loại thú vật khác nhau và nơi sinh sống của chúng. Bài thơ cho chúng ta biết việc xem tất cả các loại thú vật khác nhau tại nơi sinh sống của chúng thật là đẹp như thế nào. Bài thơ "Little Allie Alligator" kể về một con cá sấu con. Cô bé này thích nằm nghỉ suốt ngày trên một khúc gỗ. Cha của Allie tìm cách đánh thức em dậy. Ông muốn em ăn bữa cơm tối với mình. Nhưng Allie chỉ thích ngủ. Khi Allie sau cùng thức dậy, em đói bụng. Cha của em cười và nói với em là tự đi tìm thức ăn tối cho mình.

READING 2: "Can You See Them?"

English

Camouflage is the main point in this reading. It shows different animals and how they use camouflage to help themselves. Some animals use camouflage to hide from predators, while others use it to catch prey.

Spanish

El tema principal de este texto es el camuflaje. Presenta a varios animales y explica cómo usan el camuflaje en su favor. Algunos animales usan el camuflaje para esconderse de los depredadores, mientras que otros lo usan para atrapar a sus presas.

Hmong

Lub ntsiab rau zaj no yog txoj kev zais yus lub cev. Nws piav txog tej yam tsiaj txhu thiab qhia seb lawv ua li cas thiaj zais tau lawv tus kheej. Ib txhia tsiaj txhu siv txoj kev zais lawv lub cev xwv kom lwm cov tsiaj uas xav noj lawv yuav nrhiav tsis pom, es lwm cov zais lawv lub cev xwv kom lawv thiaj tom tau lwm tus tsiaj.

READING 2: "Can You See Them?"

Chinese

伪装是本文叙述的主要内容。这里讲述了不同的动物如何运用各自的伪装手段来帮助自己。有些动物运用伪装来躲避掠食者，而有些动物则运用伪装来掠食。

Cambodian

ការលាក់ខ្លួន គឺជាចំណុចសំខាន់នៅក្នុងអំណាននេះ ។ វាបង្ហាញពីសត្វផ្សេងៗគ្នា និងវិធីដែលពួកវាប្រើប្រាស់ការលាក់ខ្លួនដើម្បីជួយខ្លួន វា ។ សត្វមួយចំនួន ប្រើប្រាស់ការលាក់ខ្លួនដើម្បីលាក់ខ្លួនពីពេជ្ឈឃាត ហើយមួយចំនួនទៀតប្រើប្រាស់ដើម្បីចាប់សត្វល្អិតៗជាចំណី ។

Vietnamese

Ngụy trang là điểm chính của bài viết này. Nó cho biết những động vật khác nhau sử dụng ngụy trang để tự giúp mình như thế nào. Có loài động vật sử dụng ngụy trang để trốn khỏi dã thú, trong khi một số loài khác lại dùng nó để bắt mồi.

READING 3: "How Do They Grow?"

English

This reading describes how a butterfly and frog grow and change over their lifetimes. The butterfly starts out as an egg, which then hatches and becomes a caterpillar. The caterpillar then surrounds itself in a chrysalis before finally becoming a butterfly. The frog also starts out as an egg but quickly turns into a tadpole. As the tadpole grows legs and moves on land, it becomes a frog.

Spanish

Este texto describe los cambios que experimentan una mariposa y una rana en el transcurso de sus vidas. La mariposa empieza siendo un huevo, que se desarrolla hasta convertirse en oruga. Luego, la oruga se recubre con una crisálida, para finalmente convertirse en mariposa. La rana también empieza siendo un huevo, pero rápidamente se convierte en renacuajo. Cuando le crecen patas y comienza a andar por la tierra, el renacuajo se convierte en rana.

Hmong

Zaj no piav seb ib tug npauj npaim thiab ib tug qav loj hlob thiab pauv li cas hauv lawv lub neej. Tus npauj npaim pib ua ib le qe, uas daug thiab rais los mus ua ib tug kab ntsig. Tus kab ntsig uas tsev ces pauv los ua tus npauj npaim. Tus qav pib ua ib lub qe uas pauv los ua me nyuam qav. Thaum tus me nyuam qav pib tuaj ceg thiab khiav mus nyob nruab nqhuab, nws rais los ua ib tug qav.

READING 3: "How Do They Grow?"

Chinese

本文介绍蝴蝶和青蛙的生长和变化。蝴蝶起初是一颗卵，然后孵化变成毛毛虫。毛毛虫用茧把自己包起来，直到最后变成蝴蝶。青蛙起初也是一颗卵，但很快就变成了蝌蚪。当蝌蚪长出腿并能够在陆地上移动时，它就变成了青蛙。

Cambodian

អំណាននេះរៀបរាប់ពីរបៀបដែលមេអំបៅ និងកង្កែបរីកធំធាត់ និងផ្លាស់ប្ដូរជីវិតរបស់ពួកវា ។ មេអំបៅចាប់ផ្ដើមជាស៊ុតមួយ ដែលបន្ទាប់មកញាស់ និងក្លាយទៅជាដង្កូវមេអំបៅ ។ បន្ទាប់មក ដង្កូវមេអំបៅរុំព័ទ្ធខ្លួនឯងក្នុងដឹកឡើ មុនពេលក្លាយទៅជាមេអំបៅនាទីបំផុត ។ កង្កែបក៏ចាប់ផ្ដើមជាស៊ុតមួយផងដែរ តែប្ដូរទៅជាកូនកុកយ៉ាងឆាប់រហ័ស ។ ពេលដែលកូនកុករីកធំធាត់ជេីង និងផើរលើដី វាក៏ក្លាយទៅជាកង្កែប ។

Vietnamese

Bài viết này miêu tả con bướm và con ếch lớn lên và thay đổi trong suốt cuộc đời của chúng như thế nào. Bướm bắt đầu là trứng, sau đó nở ra và trở thành sâu bướm. Sâu bướm sau đó tự bao quanh mình thành nhộng trước khi cuối cùng trở thành bướm. Ếch cũng bắt đầu là trứng nhưng sau đó nhanh chóng trở thành con nòng nọc. Khi nòng nọc mọc chân và di chuyển lên bờ, nó trở thành con ếch.

READING 1: "On Your Bike, Get Set, Donate!"

English

This reading tells of the many organizations that take old bikes, fix them up, and donate them. Along with donating the refurbished bikes, they also donate helmets and give bicycle safety lessons. Bikes are even sent to other countries where they are needed. Even children fix up their bicycles to help in this great effort.

Spanish

Este texto trata sobre las muchas organizaciones que reparan bicicletas viejas y las dan en donación. Además de donar las bicicletas reacondicionadas, también donan cascos y dan clases de seguridad para ciclistas. Incluso envían bicicletas a otros países, donde sea que las necesiten. Hasta los niños reparan sus bicicletas para contribuir a este gran esfuerzo.

Hmong

Zaj no piav txog ntau lub koom haum uas yuav cov lub luv thij qub, muab kho, thiab pub rau lwm tus neeg. Tsis yog lawv pub cov lub luv thij uas tau muab kho xwb, lawv kuj pab pub cov kaus mom tawv thiab qhia tib neeg tej kev cai caij lub luv thij kom thiaj tsis raug xwm txheej. Yeej xa cov lub luv thij rau lwm lub teb chaws uas xav tau. Cov me nyuam kuj pab kho lawv cov lub luv thij kom muab kev pab li no thiab.

READING 1: "On Your Bike, Get Set, Donate!"

Chinese

本文讲述了许多组织收购旧自行车，将他们修好，然后再捐赠出去的事迹。除捐赠经翻新的自行车以外，他们还捐赠头盔，并讲授行车安全课程。自行车甚至被送往有需要的其它国家。就连孩子们也自己动手修理自行车，为此类慈善活动贡献出自己的一份力量。

Cambodian

អំណាននេះរៀបរាប់ប្រាប់ពីអង្គការជាច្រើនដែលទទួលយកកង់ចាស់ៗ និងជួសជុលពួកវាឡើងវិញ ហើយបរិច្ចាគពួកវា ។ ស្របជាមួយការបរិច្ចាគកង់ដែលបានជួសជុលឡើងវិញនោះ ពួកគេក៏បានបរិច្ចាគមួកសុវត្ថិភាព និងផ្តល់ឲ្យនូវមេរៀនសុវត្ថិភាពកង់ផងដែរ ។ កង់ជាច្រើន ក៏ត្រូវបានធ្វើទៅកាន់ប្រទេសផ្សេងទៀត ដែលត្រូវការពួកវាផងដែរ ។ សូម្បីតែកុមារ ក៏ជួសជុលកង់របស់ពួកគេ ដើម្បីជួយដល់កិច្ចខិតខំប្រឹងប្រែងដ៏ធំធេងនេះផងដែរ ។

Vietnamese

Bài viết này kể về nhiều tổ chức nhận xe đạp cũ, sửa chúng rồi đem tặng. Cùng với việc tặng xe đạp đã tân trang lại, họ còn tặng mũ bảo hiểm và dạy các bài học an toàn khi đạp xe. Họ còn gửi xe đạp tới những nước đang cần xe. Ngay cả các em nhỏ cũng sửa xe đạp của mình để góp phần vào nỗ lực lớn lao này.

READING 2: "Scientists and Crows"

English

This reading questions whether animals are smart or if they are just born with instinct. Scientists in this reading study crows. The scientists are trying to figure out if crows use instinct or if they can really solve problems. Scientists still need to do more tests to come up with a conclusion.

Spanish

Este texto se cuestiona si los animales son inteligentes o sólo actúan por instinto. Los científicos de este texto estudiaron a los cuervos y están tratando de determinar si los cuervos actúan por instinto o si realmente pueden resolver problemas. Para llegar a una conclusión, los científicos necesitan hacer aun más pruebas.

Hmong

Zaj no nug seb cov tsiaj txhu puas txawj ntse los sis lawv yug los es paub li ub li no xwb. Cov kws kawm txuj ci hauv zaj no kawm txog cov uab lag. Cov kws kawm txuj ci tab tom kawm seb cov uab lag puas lam paub ua ub ua no xwb los sis lawv puas txawj kawm kho tej teeb meem. Cov kws kawm txuj ci tseem yuav tau kuaj xyuas ntxiv kom thiaj paub yog li cas tiag.

READING 2: "Scientists and Crows"

Chinese

这篇文章就动物到底是具有聪明智慧还是只具有天生的本能进行了讨论。在文中，科学家们对乌鸦进行了研究。他们试图弄明白乌鸦的行为是出于本能还是它们真的会解决问题。要得出结论，科学家们还需要做更多的实验。

Cambodian

អំណាននេះ ចោទសួរថាតើសត្វមានភាពវ័យឆ្លាតដែលរួមអត់ ឬថាតើពួកវាកើតមកដោយមានសភាវគតិដែលរួមអត់ ។

អ្នកវិទ្យាសាស្ត្រនៅក្នុងអំណាន នេះ សិក្សាអំពីសត្វក្អែក ។ អ្នកវិទ្យាសាស្ត្រកំពុងព្យាយាមកំណត់ថាតើ សត្វក្អែកប្រើប្រាស់សភាវគតិ ឬថាតើពួកវាពិតជាអាចដោះស្រាយបញ្ហាបានមែន ។ អ្នកវិទ្យាសាស្ត្រនៅតែត្រូវការធ្វើពិសោធន៍បន្ថែមទៀតដើម្បីស្វែងរកការសន្និដ្ឋាន ។

Vietnamese

Bài viết này đặt câu hỏi rằng động vật là loài thông minh hay chúng chỉ được sinh ra với bản năng. Các nhà khoa học trong bài này nghiên cứu loài quạ. Các nhà khoa học cố tìm hiểu xem quạ dùng bản năng hay chúng có thể thực sự giải quyết các vấn đề. Các nhà khoa học còn cần làm thêm các thử nghiệm nữa mới đi đến kết luận.

READING 3: "A Story to Tell"

English

This reading tells us about things Native Americans from Texas and other parts of the United States make, such as cornhusk dolls, teepees, pottery, clothing, baskets, and quilts. These items tell us stories—they tell us something of the history of the people who made them.

Spanish

Esta lectura trata sobre los objetos fabricados por los nativos norteamericanos de Texas y de otras partes de los Estados Unidos, como muñecos de chala, tipis, alfarería, ropa, canastos y edredones. Estos objetos nos cuentan historias; nos cuentan algo de la historia de las personas que los fabricaron.

Hmong

Zaj no qhia peb txog tej yam uas cov Neeg Khab los ntawm Texas thiab lwm qhov chaw hauv Teb Chaws Amelikas ua xws li, me nyuam roj hmab, tsev pheeb suab, twj tais uas yog muab av puab, khaub ncaws, pob tawb thiab pam. Txhua yam khoom no qhia tau tej zaj dab neeg rau peb—tej no qhia peb txog cov neeg uas ua tej ntawd zaj keeb kwm.

READING 3: "A Story to Tell"

Chinese

这篇读物介绍了得克萨斯和美国其他地方原住民制作的物品，比如玉米壳娃娃、圆锥形帐篷、陶器、服装、篮子和被子。这些物品告诉我们许多故事 – 它们告诉我们其制造者的一些历史。

Cambodian

អំណាននេះរៀបរាប់ពីអ្វី១ទាំងអស់ដែលជនជាតិអាមេរិកាំងដើមមកពីរដ្ឋតិចសាស់ និងបើកផ្សេងទៀតនៃសហរដ្ឋអាមេរិកធ្វើដូចជា តុក្កតាសំបកពោត រូបទីបី គ្រឿងស្គូន ក្រណាត់ ជាល និងកម្រាលទ្រាប់ ។ វត្ថុទាំងនេះប្រាប់យើងអំពីរឿងរ៉ាវជាច្រើន – ពួកវាប្រាប់យើងអំពីអ្វី១ក្នុងប្រវត្តិសាស្ត្ររបស់មនុស្សដែលបានបង្កើតពួកវា ។

Vietnamese

Bài đọc này cho chúng ta biết về những vật dụng mà Người Mỹ Bản Xứ tại Texas và các nơi khác của Hoa Kỳ làm, chẳng hạn như các con búp bê làm bằng vỏ bắp, những cái lều kiểu người da đỏ, đồ gốm thủ công, y phục, giỏ đựng, và mền bông. Các đồ vật này cho chúng ta biết về những câu chuyện—một đôi điều về lịch sử của những người đã chế tạo ra chúng.

READING 1: "Earth and Beyond"

English

This informational reading asks and answers many questions about earth and the sky. In this reading, people learn about the moon, sun, and stars. It talks about the planets and solar system. This reading is very informative.

Spanish

Este texto informativo presenta muchas preguntas y respuestas sobre la tierra y el cielo. Este texto nos enseña sobre el sol, la luna y las estrellas. Trata sobre los planetas y el sistema solar, y es muy instructivo.

Hmong

Zaj qhia xov xwm no nug thiab teb ntau lo lus nug txog lub ntiaj teb thiab lub ntuj. Nyob hauv zaj no, tib neeg kawm txog lub hli, lub hnub, thiab cov hnub qub. Nws piav txog tag nrho cov ntiaj teb thiab lub ntuj. Zaj no yeej qhia txog ntau yam.

READING 1: "Earth and Beyond"

Chinese

这篇知识型文章提出并解答了许多有关地球及宇宙的问题。读者可从中了解到月球、太阳及星星的知识。文章介绍了行星及太阳系，极具知识性。

Cambodian

អំណានព័ត៌មាននេះ សួរ និងឆ្លើយចម្លើយជាច្រើនអំពីភពផែនដី និងមេឃ ។ នៅក្នុងអំណាននេះ មនុស្សសិក្សាពីព្រះច័ន្ទ ព្រះអាទិត្យ និងដួងតារា ។ វានិយាយអំពីភពជាច្រើន និងប្រព័ន្ធព្រះអាទិត្យ ។ អំណាននេះ ផ្តល់ឲ្យព័ត៌មានច្រើនណាស់ ។

Vietnamese

Bài viết tư liệu này hỏi và trả lời nhiều câu hỏi về trái đất và bầu trời. Trong bài viết này, con người tìm hiểu về mặt trăng, mặt trời và các ngôi sao. Nó nói về các hành tinh và thái dương hệ. Bài viết này có rất nhiều thông tin hữu ích.

READING 2: "One Moon, Many Myths"

English

This reading tells of three myths about the sun, moon, and sky. The first myth is about a girl who climbed a rainbow up to the moon. While on the moon, she beat bark until it was soft cloth. She threw the cloth all over the sky, and that is where we get clouds. The Australians tell the myth of the moon. One day Baloo, the Moon, tried to get in a canoe with two girls. Baloo fell in the water and the girls laughed. Baloo was so embarrassed that he hid in the sky. He sometimes shows his face, but then he gets embarrassed and hides again. The last myth tells of the sun and the moon. Mother Earth had two children, whom she loved very much. She sent them to the sky. The son became the sun and the daughter became the moon.

Spanish

Este texto trata sobre tres mitos acerca del sol, la luna y el cielo. El primer mito cuenta que una niña trepó por un arco iris hasta llegar a la Luna. Mientras estaba en la luna formó una tela suave con la corteza de ciertos árboles. Luego extendió la tela por todo el cielo y de ahí vienen las nubes. Los australianos cuentan el mito de la luna. Un día Baloo, la luna, intentó subirse a una canoa con dos niñas, pero cayó al agua y las niñas se rieron. Baloo sintió tanta vergüenza que se escondió en el cielo. Algunas veces se asoma, pero luego siente vergüenza y se vuelve a esconder. El último mito trata sobre el sol y la luna. La Madre Tierra tenía dos hijos, a los que quería mucho. Los envió al cielo; el hijo se convirtió en el sol y la hija en la luna.

Hmong

Zaj no piav peb zaj dab neeg txog lub hnub, lub hli thiab lub ntuj. Thawj zaj dab neeg qhia txog ib tug ntxhais uas tau nce tus zaj sawv mus rau lub hli. Thaum nyob saum lub hli, nws ntaus cov tawv ntoo txog thaum cov tawv ntoo yog ib txoj phuam mos mos. Nws pov txoj phuam rau hauv lub ntuj, ua li ces peb thiaj muaj cov huab. Cov neeg Australian qhia ib zag dab neeg txog lub hli. Muaj ib hnub Baloo tug Hli, tau sim nce mus hauv ib lub nkoj nrog ob tug ntxhais hluas. Baloo poob dej thiab ob tug ntxhais tau luag nws. Baloo txaj muag kawg nws thiaj mus nkaum saum ntuj. Tej thaum nws tawm los, tiam sis nws txawm txaj muag ces nws khiav mus nkaum dua. Zaj dab neeg kawg piav txog lub hnub thiab lub hli. Leej niam uas yog lub Ntiaj Teb muaj ob tug me nyuam uas nws hlub kawg nkaus li. Nws xa nkawd mus nyob saum ntuj. Tus tub rais los mus ua lub hnub thiab tus ntxhais rais los mus ua lub hli.

READING 2: "One Moon, Many Myths"

Chinese

本文讲述了有关太阳、月亮及天空的三个神话故事。第一篇神话故事的主人公是一个女孩，她爬上彩虹的高处，并登上了月亮。在月亮上，她将树皮敲打成松软的布料。她将这些布料撒向天空，凡是撒有布料的地方就是我们看见的云彩。澳大利亚人流传着一篇有关月亮的神话。一天，Baloo，也就是月亮，试着和两个女孩一起登上一叶独木舟。Baloo不小心跌入水中，引得两个女孩大笑。Baloo 觉得十分尴尬，便藏在了天空中。他有时露出脸庞，觉得尴尬时便再次藏起来。最后一篇神话的主人公是太阳和月亮。地球妈妈有两个自己深爱着的孩子。她将两个孩子送到了天上。儿子成了太阳，女儿成了月亮。

Cambodian

អំណាននេះរៀបរាប់ពីរឿងទាំងបីអំពីព្រះអាទិត្យ ព្រះច័ន្ទ និងមេឃ ។ រឿងទីមួយគឺអំពីក្មេងស្រីម្នាក់ ដែលបានឡើងលើឥន្ធនូទៅកាន់ព្រះច័ន្ទ ។ ពេលនៅលើព្រះច័ន្ទ នាងចាំងសំបកឈើរហូតដល់វាក្លាយជាក្រណាត់ទន់ ។ នាងបានចោលក្រណាត់នៅពេញមេឃ ហើយដែលធ្វើឲ្យយើងមានពពក ។ ជនជាតិអូស្ត្រាលីប្រាប់ពីរឿងព្រះច័ន្ទ ។ នាថ្ងៃមួយ បាលូ ដែលជាព្រះច័ន្ទ បានព្យាយាមចូលទៅកាន់ទូកថែវជាមួយក្មេងស្រីពីរនាក់ ។ បាលូ បានធ្លាក់ទៅក្នុងទឹក ហើយក្មេងស្រីទាំងនោះសើច ។ បាលូ ខ្មាសអៀនណាស់ ហើយលាក់ខ្លួននៅក្នុងមេឃ ។ ជួនកាល វាបង្ហាញមុខ តែបន្ទាប់មកវាខ្មាសអៀន ហើយលាក់ខ្លួនម្តងទៀត ។ រឿងចុងក្រោយរៀបរាប់ពីព្រះអាទិត្យ និងព្រះច័ន្ទ ។ អ្នកម្តាយដែលដឹងមានកូនពីរនាក់ ដែលគាត់ស្រឡាញ់ខ្លាំងណាស់ ។ គាត់បានបញ្ជូនពួកវាទៅកាន់លើមេឃ ។ កូនប្រុសបានក្លាយទៅជាព្រះអាទិត្យ ហើយកូនស្រីបានក្លាយទៅជាព្រះច័ន្ទ ។

Vietnamese

Bài viết này kể ba câu chuyện thần thoại về mặt trời, mặt trăng và bầu trời. Chuyện thần thoại đầu tiên là về một cô gái đã leo lên cầu vồng để lên mặt trăng. Khi ở trên mặt trăng, cô đánh tơi vỏ cây cho đến khi nó thành vải mềm. Cô tung vải khắp bầu trời và đó là nơi chúng ta có mây. Người Úc kể câu chuyện thần thoại về mặt trăng. Một hôm, mặt trăng Baloo cố gắng bước lên chiếc thuyền nhỏ với hai cô gái. Baloo ngã xuống nước và các cô gái cười lớn. Baloo xấu hổ đến nỗi phải trốn trong bầu trời. Đôi lúc Anh ta chìa khuôn mặt ra nhưng sau đó lại xấu hổ và trốn đi. Chuyện thần thoại cuối cùng kể về mặt trời và mặt trăng. Mẹ Trái Đất có hai đứa con mà bà rất yêu thương. Bà gởi chúng lên bầu trời. Người con trai đã trở thành mặt trời và người con gái trở thành mặt trăng.

READING 3: "Franklin's Dream"

English

This is a reading about a man named Franklin Chang-Diaz. After seeing *Sputnik* lift off, he dreamt of becoming an astronaut. With much studying and hard work, his dreams came true. In 1986 he was an astronaut on *Columbia*'s flight. Franklin loves looking at Earth from outer space.

Spanish

Este texto trata sobre un hombre llamado Franklin Chang-Díaz. Luego de ver el despegue del *Sputnik* soñó con convertirse en astronauta. Luego de estudiar y esforzarse mucho, sus sueños se hicieron realidad. En 1986, fue uno de los astronautas a bordo del *Columbia*. A Franklin le encanta contemplar la Tierra desde el espacio exterior.

Hmong

Nov yog ib zaj uas piav txog ib tug txiv neej hu ua Franklin Chang-Diaz. Tom qab nws pom lub dav hlau uas yas mus puag saum lub lwm ntuj hu ua *Sputnik* ya mus, nws twb xav xav ua ib tug neeg caij dav hlau mus saum ntuj li ntawd. Vim nws rau siab kawm ntawv thiab tau siv zog ua hauj lwm, nws thiaj tau ua raws li nws lub siab xav. Thaum xyoo 1986 nws yog ib tug neeg uas caij lub dav hlau *Sputnik* mus saum ntuj. Franklin nyiam saib lub ntiaj teb, Earth, thaum nws nyob puag saum qaum ntuj li ntawd.

READING 3: "Franklin's Dream"

Chinese

本文的主人公名叫张福林。在看到哥伦比亚号航天飞机发射升空后，他也梦想成为一名宇航员。经过刻苦的学习和努力，他的梦想变成了现实。他于 1986 年成为哥伦比亚号航天飞机上的一名宇航员。他非常喜欢从外太空观看地球。

Cambodian

នេះគឺជាអំណានអំពីបុរសម្នាក់ឈ្មោះ ប្រាង់គ្លីន ចាង ឌីអាស ។ បន្ទាប់ពីឃើញ *ស្ប៉ុតនីក* ចាកចេញទៅ គាត់បានសុបិន្តក្លាយជាអវកាសយានិក ។ ដោយមានការសិក្សាច្រើន និងការងារធ្ងន់ សុបិន្តរបស់បានក្លាយជាការពិត ។ ក្នុងឆ្នាំ 1986 គាត់គឺជាអវកាសយានិកនៅលើយានហោះហើរ *កូឡុំប៊ី* ។ ប្រាង់គ្លីន ចូលចិត្តសម្លឹងមើលមកពភផែនដីពីលើអវកាស ។

Vietnamese

Đây là bài viết về một người đàn ông tên là Franklin Chang-Diaz. Sau khi thấy *Sputnik* cất cánh, ông mơ ước trở thành một phi hành gia. Bằng cách học nhiều và làm việc chăm chỉ, ước mơ của ông đã trở thành hiện thực. Năm 1986, ông là phi hành gia trên chuyến bay của *Columbia*. Franklin thích nhìn về Trái Đất từ ngoài không gian.

READING 1: "Arts Festival!"

English

This reading tells about an Art Festival that is held annually in Red Tree. People make posters to advertise the festival. There is a make-your-own-puppet contest. Parents and their children take art classes together at the festival.

Spanish

Este texto trata sobre un Festival Artístico que se organiza todos los años en Red Tree. Todos hacen afiches para promocionar el festival. Hay un concurso que se trata de crear tu propia marioneta. En el festival, los padres y sus hijos participan juntos de las clases de arte.

Hmong

Zaj no piav txog ib qho Kev Ua Si Kos Duab uas lawv ua txhua txhua xyoo hauv Red Tree. Tib neeg ua cov ntawv uas qhia txog txoj kev ua si no. Yeej muaj ib qho rau yus tau ua yus ib tug me nyuam roj hmab. Niam thiab txiv thiab lawv cov me nyuam kawm tej hoob uas qhia txog kev kos duab hauv txoj kev ua si no.

READING 1: "Arts Festival!"

Chinese

本文讲述了一年一度在 Red Tree 举办的艺术节。人们用海报的方式宣传该艺术节。艺术节有一个木偶制作大赛。父母和孩子们可以在艺术节上一起参加艺术学习班。

Cambodian

អំណាននេះរៀបរាប់ប្រាប់ពីពិធីបុណ្យសិល្បៈ ដែលត្រូវបានប្រារព្ធឡើងរៀងរាល់ឆ្នាំនៅដើមឈេីក្រហម ។ ប្រជាជនធ្វើបណ្ណប្រកាស ផ្សព្វផ្សាយពិធីបុណ្យ ។ មាននូវការប្រកួតរូបអាយ៉ងធ្វើដោយខ្លួនឯងផងដែរ ។ ឪពុកម្តាយ និងកូនៗរបស់ពួកគេ ចូលរៀនថ្នាក់សិល្បៈ ទាំងអស់គ្នានៅឯពិធីបុណ្យនេះ ។

Vietnamese

Bài viết này kể về một Lễ Hội Nghệ Thuật được tổ chức hằng năm ở Red Tree. Người ta làm các tấm áp phích để quảng cáo cho lễ hội. Có một cuộc thi tự làm con rối của riêng mình. Bố mẹ và con cái họ cùng tham dự các lớp học nghệ thuật tại lễ hội.

READING 2: "How to Make Puppets"

English

This reading tells how to make a puppet. It tells what you need to make your puppet. It breaks down how to make a puppet into four steps.

Spanish

Este texto explica cómo hacer una marioneta. Detalla los elementos necesarios para armarla. Divide el proceso de creación de una marioneta en cuatro pasos.

Hmong

Zaj no piav seb yuav ua li cas thiaj ua tau ib tug me nyuam roj hmab. Zaj no qhia tias yus xav tau cov khoom zoo li cas thiaj ua tau yus tus me nyuam roj hmab. Nws qhia plaub theem uas yus yuav tsum ua kom thiaj ua tau tus me nyuam roj hmab.

READING 2: "How to Make Puppets"

Chinese

本文介绍了木偶的制作方法。文章介绍了制作木偶所需要的材料。它将木偶的制作过程分为四个步骤。

Cambodian

អំណាននេះរៀបរាប់ប្រាប់ពីរបៀបធ្វើអាយ៉ង ។ វារៀបរាប់ប្រាប់ពីអ្វីដែលអ្នកត្រូវការ ដើម្បីធ្វើអាយ៉ងរបស់អ្នក ។ វាបានបំបែករបៀបធ្វើអាយ៉ងជាបួនដំណាក់កាល ។

Vietnamese

Bài viết này nói về cách làm con rối. Nó cho biết bạn cần những gì để làm con rối cho mình. Nó chia cách làm con rối thành bốn bước.

READING 3: "The Bonnaroo Music and Arts Festival"

English

This reading is about the Bonnaroo Music and Arts Festival that takes place in Manchester, Tennessee. It lasts for four days, and nearly 65,000 adults and kids attend every summer to listen to jazz, country, and rock music. Artists also show their work and have booths where they can teach kids how to make their own art, such as T-shirts and posters. Bonnaroo even has games, rides, and a water park called Splash-a-roo with water slides. When people are hungry they can go to booths from local restaurants, and at night most people camp out under the stars.

Spanish

Esta lectura se ocupa del Festival de Música y Artes *Bonnaroo,* que tiene lugar en Manchester, Tennessee. El festival dura cuatro días y cerca de 65,000 adultos y niños participan cada año para escuchar jazz, country y rock. Algunos artistas también exponen sus obras y tienen cabinas en las que enseñan a los niños a hacer su propio arte en camisetas y carteles. Bonnaroo también tiene juegos, atracciones y un parque acuático llamado *Splash-a-roo* con toboganes de agua. Cuando las personas sienten hambre pueden ir a cabinas de restaurantes locales y, por la noche, mucha gente simplemente acampa bajo las estrellas.

Hmong

Cov lus nyeem ntawm no hais txog lub Bonnaroo Music thiab Arts Festival uas nyob rau hauv Manchester, Tennessee. Nws ua mus ntev li plaub hnub, thiab 65,000 cov neeg laus thiab menyuam yaus tau tuaj koom txhua lub caij ntuj sov los mloog rau cov nkauj jazz, country, thiab rock. Cov kws kos duab yuav nthuav lawv cov duab uas lawv tau kos thiab yuav teeb rooj los qhia cov menyuam kos lawv cov duab xws li cov tsho hnav thiab cov duab dai. Bonnaroo tseem muaj kev sib tw ua si, muaj tej yam caij ua si, thiab lub chaw ua si dej hu ua Splash-a-roo nrog cov zawv zuag dej thiab. Thaum cov neeg tshaib plab lawv mus tau rau ntawm cov rooj teeb uas cov khw hauv lub zej zog tuaj muag zaub mov noj, thiab thaum hmo ntuj ntau tus neeg pw nraum zoo hauv qab cov hnub qub.

READING 3: "The Bonnaroo Music and Arts Festival"

Chinese

这篇读物讲到有关在田纳西州的曼彻斯特举行的波纳若音乐和艺术节。这个音乐和艺术节进行 一连四天，每个夏季差不多六万五千成人和儿童到来听爵士乐、乡村音乐、摇滚乐。艺术家也展示他们的作品，在棚舍教导儿童怎样制造自己的美术品，例如，T恤和海报。波纳若其至有游戏、游乐设施、和一个有水滑道、叫 " 飞溅-A-Roo " 的水上乐园。游客饿时就光顾当地餐馆的棚舍，很多人晚上就在星光下露营。

Cambodian

អំណាននេះ គឺអំពីពិធីបុណ្យតន្ត្រីរបស់អ្នកស្ទីនស៊ីធីលីមីត ។ ក្រុមតន្ត្រីជាង១៣០ សំដែងតន្ត្រីគ្រប់ប្រភេទដូចជា រ៉ក់ ខេនទ្រី និង ប្រជាប្រិយ ព្រមទាំងរ៉េហ្គាផងដែរ ។ ពិធីបុណ្យមាននូវពិពណ៌សិល្បៈ សកម្មភាពកំសាន្ត សម្រាប់កុមារ និង ចំណីអាហារផ្សេង១ ។ តំនិតសម្រាប់ពិធីបុណ្យនេះចេញមកពីកម្មវិធីទូរស្សន៍មួយឈ្មោះថា *អ្នកស្ទីនស៊ីធីលីមីត* ។

Vietnamese

Bài này nói về âm nhạc Bonnaroo và Lễ hội Nghệ thuật diễn ra tại Manchester, Tennessee. Lễ hội kéo dài bốn ngày, và có gần 65.000 người lớn và trẻ em tham dự mỗi mùa hè để nghe nhạc jazz, nhạc đồng quê, và nhạc rock. Nghệ sĩ cũng trình diễn tác phẩm của họ và có gian hàng nơi họ có thể dạy cho trẻ em làm thế nào để thực hiện nghệ thuật của riêng mình như áo t-shirt và áp phích. Bonnaroo thậm chí còn có các trò chơi, du hành, và có một công viên nước được gọi là Splash-a-roo trượt nước. Khi thấy đói, họ có thể vào các gian trong các nhà hàng ăn địa phương, và ban đêm hầu hết mọi người ra cắm trại dưới trời đầy sao.

GRAPHIC ORGANIZERS

Main Idea/ Supporting Details Chart

Main Idea

Supporting Details

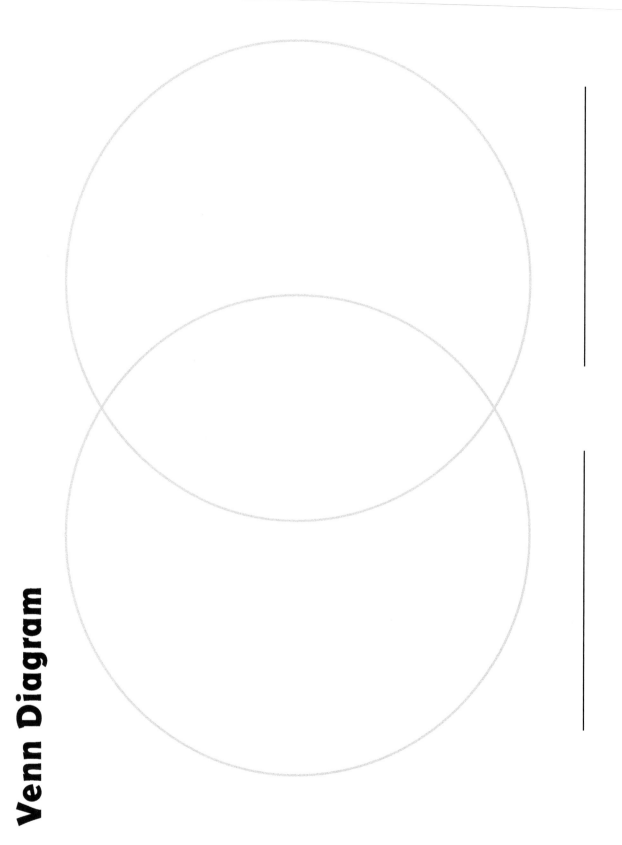

Venn Diagram

Prediction Chart

What I Predict	What Happens

Sequence of Events Chart

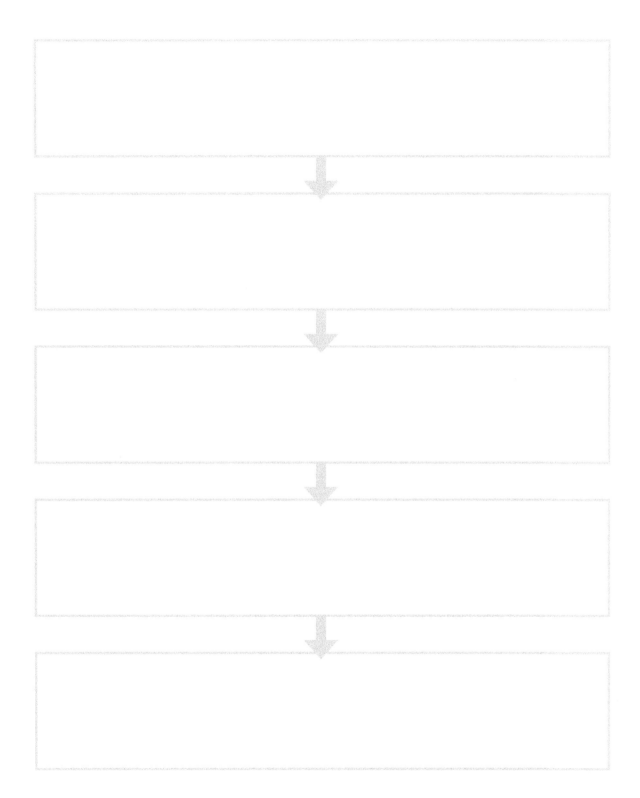

Name _____ Date _____

KWL Chart

K- What I Know	W- What I Want to Know	L- What I Learned

5 W Chart

Who?

What?

Where?

When?

Why?

5 W Organizer

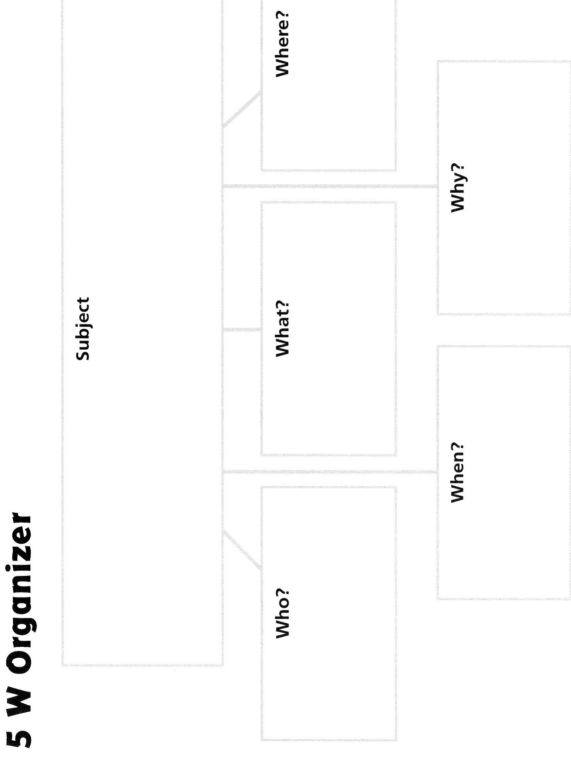

Subject

Where?

Why?

What?

When?

Who?

Cause and Effect Chart

CAUSE **EFFECT**

Why did it happen?	What happened?

Why did it happen?	What happened?

Why did it happen?	What happened?

Why did it happen?	What happened?

T-Chart

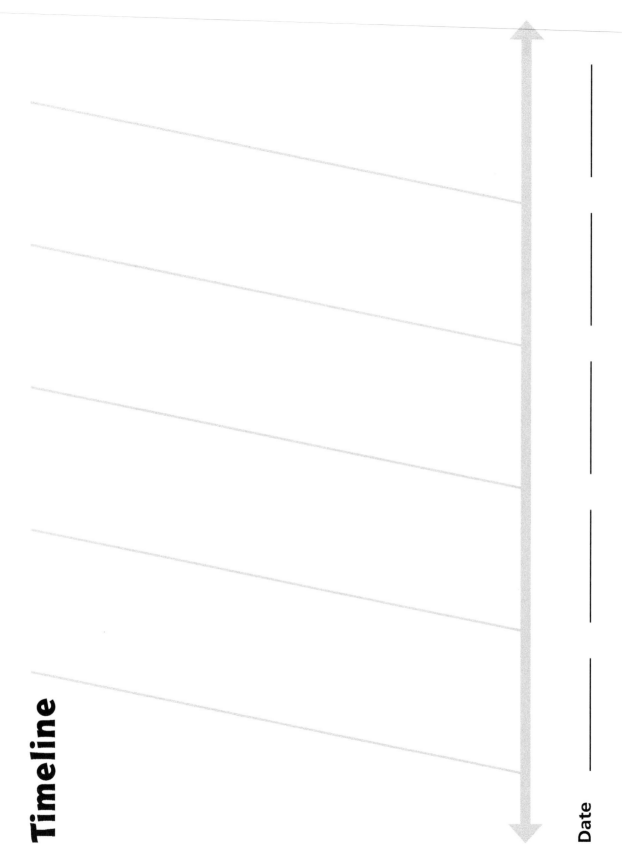

Timeline

Date

Story Map 1

Characters	Setting

Beginning

Middle

End

Three-Column Chart

Name _____ Date _____

Word Web

Character Trait Web

Trait

_____

_____

Example

_____

_____

_____

Trait

_____

_____

Example

_____

_____

_____

Character

Trait

_____

_____

Example

_____

_____

_____

Trait

_____

_____

Example

_____

_____

_____

FLUENCY

The Development of Reading Fluency

What Is Fluency?

Fluency is one of the five key components of reading proficiency, along with phonemic awareness, phonics, vocabulary, and comprehension. Fluency is generally defined as the ability to read text both quickly and accurately with appropriate expression. Up until the last decade or so, fluency was often addressed sporadically, with most attention directed to the other components of reading proficiency. Now, development of fluency is seen as very important because there is a close relationship among word recognition, comprehension, and fluent reading. Fluent readers, in contrast to nonfluent readers, do not have to focus most on decoding words. Their higher level of automatic word recognition, ability to read in meaningful "chunks," and sense of prosody allow them to direct their attention to the understanding of the text, to bring to bear their prior knowledge to the ideas in that text, and therefore to construct meaning.

Fluency happens gradually over time, through multiple opportunities for focused practice. It is important to realize that there is no one magic moment when fluency is "done," as readers' degree of fluency will change, depending on factors such as the genre they are reading, their familiarity with the words and topics, their amount of accumulated practice in reading text, and whether they are reading aloud or silently.

Most beginning readers of English, because they are just learning to connect sounds to letters and to blend letter sounds into words, read slowly and laboriously. They tend to read word for word with no expression or sense of word and sentence boundaries. Helping readers with words in isolation is important but not sufficient in terms of fluency development. Students need focused instruction and fluency practice using connected text.

What Are the Elements of Fluency Development?

Modeling

In order to become fluent readers, students need exposure to systematic modeling of fluent reading. By demonstrating what fluent reading is, teachers show how the reader's voice helps make sense of written text. Daily reading aloud to students, with attention to pronunciation, phrasing, and expression, helps them understand what a fluent reader sounds like. For the primary grades, the use of big books, texts on transparencies, and texts on posters or chart paper helps focus students' attention on the elements of fluency. As teachers read the words aloud, they use pointers or their fingers to show where and how they pause, and when they raise or lower their voices.

Text Accessibility

It is very important that students interact with texts at a level appropriate for fluency development. *Independent level text* refers to text that is relatively easy for the reader. The reader is in a comfort zone, and has difficulty with no more than one in twenty words (approximately 95% success). *Instructional level text* refers to text that is generally manageable but also somewhat challenging. The reader has difficulty with no more than one in ten words (approximately 90% success). *Frustration level text* refers to text that is too challenging for the reader's current level of development. The reader has difficulty with more than one in ten words (less than 90% success). For the purposes of fluency, students should have multiple opportunities to read text that is at their independent reading level, text that they can read with a success rate of approximately 95%. In many classrooms, teachers employ a mix of independent level text and instructional level text work. Students are allowed to self-select material at their independent reading level to read to the teacher, but they work on fluency with instructional level text only after extensive exposure to and work with that text. For example, they may have focused for some time on a combination of vocabulary development, phonics, or comprehension activities related to the instructional level text first.

Repeated Reading Research has consistently shown that repeated reading of the same text is an effective way to foster fluency development. There are several procedures teachers can use to provide these multiple opportunities for oral reading. These include one-on-one student-teacher reading, peer partner reading, choral reading, reader's theater, and recording-assisted reading.

In *student-teacher reading*, the teacher works one-on-one with the student. The teacher models the reading first, and then the student reads the text. As the student reads, the teacher provides help and feedback. The student rereads the text three to four times.

In *peer partner reading*, students work with each other. (1) For paired reading, the teacher may decide to put a more fluent reader together with a less fluent reader. The more fluent student reads the text first, and then the less fluent reader reads it back. The more fluent reader may help with word recognition and phrasing, as well as provide encouragement. (2) In another kind of paired reading, students of the same ability, having heard the teacher model the text, take turns reading the text to each other, up to three times each. They may fill out a short feedback form such as the Peer Partner Checklist on page 160. (3) In yet another form of peer reading, students form small groups and take turns reading to each other. One group member reads a portion of text as the rest of the group listens. Then the group member reads each sentence and has the rest of the group echo-read after each sentence. The procedure is repeated for each group member, with another portion of the text read each time. When everyone has finished their portions of the text, the group reads the whole text together in unison.

In *choral reading*, teachers read from a big book or other text that all students can see at the same time. The teacher chooses a text at the independent reading level of the majority of students, and models the reading. Then the teacher reads the text again as students read aloud at the same time, three to five times.

In *reader's theater*, students use repeated reading of text as a means to an end—the expressive classroom performance of a scene related to a text students have studied earlier. The teacher, with or without student participation, chooses a meaningful dialogue-rich portion of text, and then provides students with scripts for rehearsal. Students prepare for their roles by repeatedly practicing their lines so that they can read them smoothly and expressively in their live performance. See an example of a reader's theater script on page 162.

In *recording-assisted reading*, students first listen to an audio source (e.g., CD, video) and then echo-read or simultaneously read the text along with the recording.

Silent Reading Development of fluency is most effective when teachers spend class time working with nonfluent students directly, engaging in such activities such as those described above. Modeling and explicit instruction in word recognition, phrasing, and reading rate are very important for struggling readers. These students tend to benefit less from independent silent reading in the classroom because they do not yet have the automaticity, phrasing, and reading speed they need to do so. Many teachers, however, have built in time for independent reading using such systems as Sustained Silent Reading (SSR) or Drop Everything and Read (DEAR). During this scheduled independent reading time, students with few reading issues can read independently, and students with reading problems can work directly with the teacher in a separate area of the classroom.

This is not to say that struggling students should never read silently. If they have finished a class activity or a test early, they could certainly take advantage of that time to read something at their independent reading level. Or they could read silently for extra points during lunchtime, or in an after-school reading club. All students should be encouraged to read more as much as possible, especially at home.

How Is Progress in Fluency Development Measured?

Every struggling reader has individual issues. Students from different countries who are just learning English have many adjustments to make that other native but struggling readers do not have. For example, some nonnative speakers may be accustomed to reading from right to left, or vertically rather than horizontally. Some may know different alphabetic systems, or none at all. Some may have difficulty with distinguishing and producing sounds that are not present in their native languages. It is only logical, then, to assume that these students will progress more slowly in fluency development than native speakers do.

Progress in fluency can be measured both informally and formally. For example, for informal assessment, teachers may circulate around the room while students are reading aloud to each other. They may fill in a checklist (p. 160), use a simple rubric (p. 161), or take notes on several readers as they walk around the room. If teachers do this every day, they can consistently cover all of their students, a few at a time. Teachers may also ask students to read text into a tape recorder from time to time. Some teachers use miscue analysis, keep running records, or use an Informal Reading Inventory (IRI).

In formal assessment, teachers look for targeted improvement in reading rate, in phrasing, in expression, and in comprehension while reading aloud. They use timed readings to compare students' performances, calculating the number of words read correctly per minute. These results are often compared to any one of a number of published oral reading fluency norms or standards, such as Deno's Curriculum-Based Measurement/Oral Reading Fluency assessment (CBM/ORF), Good and Kaminski's Dynamic Indicators of Basic Early Literacy Skills (DIBELS), or Johns and Lenski's Basic Reading Inventory (BRI). It is important to remember that these norms are not necessarily a reliable indication of overall performance for nonnative speakers of English, due to their native language backgrounds and developing levels of English. Teachers can more accurately measure the progress of these students by comparing each student's previous performances against the latest performance.

Words Correct Per Minute (WCPM) Calculation This procedure
is used with one-minute timed readings. Errors are subtracted from the total number of words read in one minute to arrive at the number of words correct per minute.

1. For formal assessment, choose a passage equal to or slightly above the word counts used on the unit fluency pages in the Student's Book. The passage should be one students have worked with before.
2. Working one on one, have the student read the text aloud for exactly one minute. As the student reads, mark the number of errors (substitution of a word, omission of a word, insertion of a new word, reversal of two words, repetition of a word).
3. After one minute, stop the student. Count up the number of words read.
4. Count up the number of errors made during the reading.
5. Subtract the number of errors from the total number of words read during the minute. The result is the number of words correct per minute.
6. Use this procedure several times throughout the year to measure the student's growth in fluency.

Peer Partner Checklist

These checklists can be photocopied and distributed to be used with appropriate Fluency Activities.

I noticed that _____, my partner

After 2nd reading	After 3rd reading
☐	☐ remembered more words
☐	☐ read faster
☐	☐ read more smoothly
☐	☐ read with more expression

I noticed that _____, my partner

After 2nd reading	After 3rd reading
☐	☐ remembered more words
☐	☐ read faster
☐	☐ read more smoothly
☐	☐ read with more expression

Rubric Describing Oral Fluency

Ability Level	Description
4	Student consistently reads with appropriate speed, phrasing, expression, and accuracy
3	Student often reads with close to average speed, phrasing, expression, and accuracy; attends to punctuation
2	Student often reads in short phrases but sometimes word for word; sometimes ignores punctuation; low expressivity
1	Student reads haltingly word for word; frequent long pauses between words; frequently ignores sentence boundaries
0	Student is unable to associate English sounds and spellings; cannot recognize words, word and sentence boundaries, punctuation

Sample Reader's Theater Script

NARRATOR

Jessie came out of the art room as the other girls were talking.

CARLA

Hey, Jessie! Casey wants to ask you something.

CASEY

I need your help.

NARRATOR

Jessie was puzzled.

JESSIE

Why should I help you?

CASEY

I'm sorry I was mean to you.
But, if you help me with science, I'll help you with basketball.

JESSIE

Why?

CASEY

Because if I don't do better in science class, I will be off the basketball team.

DAMARIS

Come on. You two can help each other. Everybody will win.

CARLA

It's worth a try. Okay?

JESSIE

Okay. We can try to help each other.

from *Everybody Wins* by Pamela Walker, © Pearson Education

Sample Graph of Student Progress: Grade 3

Adding on a car to the train each time a student progresses in fluency during evaluation provides evidence of growth.

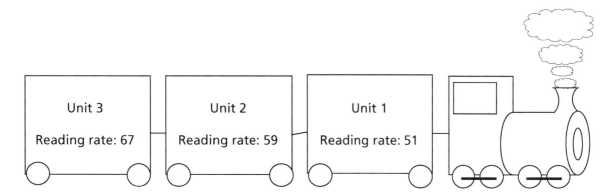

Units 1–6

This Activity is to be used for Fluency Activities 5, 8, 11 in all units.

Have students choose and practice reading texts from magazines or books. Then sit with each student to evaluate progress. Do this by listening and timing the student and noting any miscues. Let the student read the passage several times. Note the student's improvement in time and accuracy each time he/she rereads the passage. Let him or her compare the first and last reading to see the improvement.

Students enjoy seeing their progress. You could use a paper "reading train" to visually represent the student's progress. An additional train car is attached to the train engine each time the student advances in reading time and accuracy. See page 163.